Miniature Donk

Miniature Donkeys

Miniature Donkeys book for care, health, diet, training and costs.

By

Paul Chester

ALL RIGHTS RESERVED. This book contains material protected under International and Federal Copyright Laws and Treaties.

Any unauthorized reprint or use of this material is strictly prohibited. No part of this book may be reproduced or transmitted in any form or by any means, electronic, mechanical or otherwise, including photocopying or recording, or by any information storage and retrieval system without express written permission from the author.
Copyright © 2017
Published by: Zoodoo Publishing

Table of Contents

Table of Contents 3

Introduction 4

Chapter 1. Miniature Donkey Basics 6

Chapter 2. The Miniature Donkey as a Pet 10

Chapter 3. Buying Your Miniature Donkey 19

Chapter 4. General Care 31

Chapter 5. Feeding Your Miniature Donkey 41

Chapter 6. Training Your Miniature Donkey 58

Chapter 7. The Health Of Your Pet Donkey 63

Chapter 8. Miniature Donkey Reproduction 86

Chapter 9. Final Thoughts 99

Introduction

To most people, the donkey is an animal that has long ears and brays, but you can also recognize them by their gray or brown coat, (although they do come in other more "sporty" colors) a light nose and belly, a black cross on the back and shoulders, a short, thin, upright mane and a tail that is tufted at the end. The hooves of the donkey are small and box-shaped, and much more elastic than those of their cousin, the horse.

The donkey probably has more names than any other species in the equine family. The Latin name is Equus Asinus or Ass – with the male of the species being a Jack (hence the term Jack Ass). The female is a Jennet or Jenny. The donkey was originally an English name for the Ass taken from "dun-key", meaning a small dun or gray colored animal.

Besides having a lot of names, the donkey comes in about as many different sizes, shapes, breeds, and colors as the horse. Visit one of the many donkey and mule shows across the country and you will see four basic size groups: Miniature– up to 36" tall at the withers; standard – 36 to 48" tall; and large standard – 48" to 56". The mammoth – or Jack Stock is over 56". Within those sizes, you will see many colors, gray, browns, blacks, reds, and even spots. In addition, you will see many body types from deer-like and graceful to strong and sturdy; something for every job or personal reference.

As Betsy Hutchin's states in The Donkey's & Mule as a Backyard Hobby, "The most enjoyable thing about donkeys as members of the equine world is the fact that they are exceptionally loving, almost in the same manner as a dog. They love to be touched and no amount of playing or loving will spoil them for work. They are highly intelligent.

For some reason, rumors to the contrary have always existed, but all one has to do is own a donkey to know that these are not true. They also have a definite sense of humor, sometimes mischief, and a great love of human company. All in all, whether you ride or drive your donkey, or just love him, he is an unexcelled pet in the large animal category."

Please note that for ease we shall refer to the donkey as 'he', although there are female variations.

Chapter 1. Miniature Donkey Basics

If you're new to miniature donkeys, you should know the basics:

- Jennet: A female donkey.

- Jack: An unaltered male donkey who has superior conformation, overall build, disposition and pedigree, which makes him a candidate for becoming a quality herdsire.

- Gelding: A male donkey that has been castrated so that he cannot, will not, and does not want to reproduce. (Geldings make the BEST and most economical pets!)

- Foal: This is a baby donkey from the time it is born until the time it is weaned from its mother.

- Weanling: A young donkey that has been separated from its mother (a weanling will be anywhere from 4-5 months old to one year old)

- Yearling: A young donkey that is between one and two years of age.

- A miniature donkey does not reach maturity until the age of 3. This is important to know! Jennets should never be bred prior to the age of 3 years old because of this very reason.

They need time to grow and mature, both physically and mentally before breeding.

- A miniature donkey jennet will carry her foal for 11 to 13 months on average.

- A miniature donkey foal averages between 19 & 25 pounds at birth, and between 18 & 25 inches in height.

- Foals are weaned from their mothers from 4 to 6 months of age.

- The most common color for a miniature donkey is gray-dun. Other colors include various shades of brown, black, spotted, red and frosted spotted white. A donkey listed as having MSF (masked spotting factor) means the body color is solid but the donkey has a white blaze on its face. A donkey listed as having NLP (no light points) means the donkey does not have the typical white belly, white muzzle, white around the eyes, or white inside the ears.

- The life expectancy for miniature donkeys is anywhere from 25 - 35+ years, making donkey ownership an important lifelong commitment!

- The average adult donkey will weigh between 250-350 pounds.

Can I have just one donkey?

Generally, no. Miniature donkeys are very social animals. They buddy up in pairs, or even in groups of three, and will go to the earth's end to stay with their best friends. We've found they get very upset if separated, so we try to keep the girls with their best buddy, or buddies, at all times if at all possible. Because of this strong need to be with another equine, we will not knowingly sell one single, lone donkey without an equine companion(s) waiting for them at your home.

Donkeys thrive when allowed to live with other donkeys. When at all possible we try to find homes for our foals in pairs. Although rare, we have had a few people manage to get one donkey to buddy up with a pony or horse. This seems to work only when they are the only two animals present. If you take one donkey into a situation with several horses or ponies and expect that donkey to buddy up with one of them, you will be disappointed. A single, lone donkey is a lonely donkey and should be avoided if at all possible.

Habitat

Wild donkeys are only found in deserts and savannahs in northern Africa from Morocco to Somalia, in the Arabian Peninsula and in the Middle East. Domesticated donkeys, on the other hand, are found all over the world, but prefer dry, warm areas. The Abyssinian donkey, for example, is bred in Ethiopia, according to Oklahoma State University, while the Anatolia donkey is bred in Turkey. One species, the kiang or Tibetan wild ass is found in China, northern parts of Pakistan, India, Nepal and Bhutan.

Chapter 2. The Miniature Donkey as a Pet

Do you want a faithful companion for life? Miniature donkeys are becoming more beloved as pets nowadays because of their life expectancy of approximately 25 to 30+ years. However, some reach close to 50 years ,which practically matches the number of years of human beings. They are faithful, affectionate, intelligent, helpful and easy to train.

The miniature donkey can be a great pet to have and completely affectionate, warm and trustworthy around children and often serves as a companion that lasts through time. They are most helpful to the elderly and the handicapped, are usually trained to pull a cart or a wagon, very dependable, and could also be conditioned to carry weight and cargo of up to 100 pounds.

Since miniature donkeys are herd animals, they effectively thrive in a small pasture with other donkeys and animals. They could also guard animals in the farm to protect newborn animals from predators like coyotes and wild dogs. These sweet and loving animals respond well to correct training, care and attention so it is best to prepare everything first before having them around the house. They can be companions and best friends for life, dearly beloved and trusted pets to have.

How to raise a donkey as a pet

Step 1 : Read as many books on choosing and raising donkeys as you can find. Try your local library if you don;t want to buy them. If they have none available, ask about inter-library loan options.

Step 2 : Think carefully about what type of donkey you want. If you have no experience raising or training equine, you may want to choose an adult donkey as your first pet instead of an untrained youngster. Jacks should also be avoided if what you want is a pet only. Also consider the price and personality of the animal.

Step 3 : Build an adequate shelter for your pet donkey. It does not need to be elaborate. Make sure it is weather resistant for your location including the wind and snow-bearing weather conditions.

Step 4 : Enclose the shelter with a fence system. Tightly stretched, dive-barbed wire should be avoided, especially if you have a breeding jack. Try to use chain link or horse fence and allow as much space as possible for your donkey to exercise and graze.

Step 5 : Feed your donkey properly to avoid illness and excess weight gain. Plain grass type hay is the best option, followed by alfalfa cubes if hay is in short supply. Occasional oat grain is suitable but try to avoid corn unless it is winter time and mixed with oats since it is high in carbohydrates and fattening.

Step 6 : Provide fresh, clean drinking water at all times. Place a salt and mineral block where it is accessible to the animal.

Step 7 : Check the donkey's hoofs frequently and have them trimmed as needed. Try to avoid having him shod unless the farrier advises it. Provide other preventative medical care such as worming and vaccinations as per your veterinarian.

Step 8 : Play with your pet donkey often so he gets plenty of attention and exercise. Groom him as needed with a good brush, and trim his shaggy coat with electric clippers if it is extremely hot outside. Blanket him if the weather is excessively cold.

Settling your donkeys into their new home

It is important to take things slowly and not rush your donkeys, as transportation, change of environment and change of companions can be very stressful for them. It is very important that you do all you can to settle your new donkeys in as calmly and quietly as possible. It can take weeks and sometimes months for donkeys to really settle into new surroundings, and during this time they can be more prone to serious conditions such as hyperlipemia.

Donkeys can be territorial and new arrivals should be carefully introduced to any existing donkeys or other equines. Ideally, keep the new and existing donkeys alongside each other but separated by a fence, either permanent or electric, for a week or two to monitor their behavior towards each other. It is important to allow new donkeys time to explore their new home and settle in before allowing the new and old to mix. Observe their behavior towards each other and, when you're sure that they are calm and relaxed in each other's company, allow them access to each other.

If you have any doubts about their behavior and acceptance of each other, then keep them living alongside each other, but not together, for a while longer.

When the new and existing donkeys first start mixing, ensure that they are supervised, that there is no competition for food, space or shelter, and that they have plenty of space to avoid each other if they wish. This will help avoid potential conflicts in the crucial early days.

It's also important to take special care of small pets such as dogs, cats, poultry, goats, sheep or lambs; donkeys are territorial by nature, and some donkeys will chase smaller animals. Supervise interactions between donkeys and small stock; if possible, avoid direct contact between them. Some donkeys do live happily with other livestock but it is difficult to know which donkeys will accept the presence of chickens, etc, and which donkeys will attack and chase them.

If your donkeys do share their environment with small stock, make sure there are safe areas or an escape route where the smaller livestock can avoid unwanted attention from the donkeys. For safety, an adult should always accompany young children into the donkeys' field.

In the first few weeks :

- Take time to get to know your donkeys.

- Spend time observing their behavior so you can establish their behavior patterns and will be able to spot subtle changes.

- Daily grooming and spending time with your donkeys will help them to feel more at home and stimulate them mentally, as well.

However, don't be tempted to try and do too much too soon. It may be better to wait a week or two before picking up their feet if they need time to get to know you. Don't be tempted to take them for a walk outside the safety of their field until you have done some leading training in their safe field and stable environment, and then only go for small, easy walks to help build their confidence and yours.

Riding, driving or working with your donkeys

Before riding, driving or working your donkeys, take into consideration their age (which should ideally be between 4 and 25 years), build, conformation and temperament.

If you are unsure of what you are looking for, ask the advice of a professional.

Here are some general guidelines:

- Always get a vet to check that your donkeys are physically fit to be ridden.

- Do not attempt to work your donkeys until they have reached the age of four. It is not until then that the bones are fully developed. Donkeys learn by gradual, progressive repetition.

- An average donkey of approximately 11 hands high or 160 kg should not carry more than 50 kg (8 stone) on its back, and the rider must always wear a well-fitted skull cap or riding hat that conforms to current safety standards, along with boots that have a flat sole and low heel.

- We recommend that a donkey pull no more than twice its body weight on flat, level ground, including the weight of a well-balanced and maintained vehicle.

- Always ensure both handler and donkey have received adequate training before attempting to ride or drive.

- Ensure that an inexperienced rider always has an assistant walking beside them, and never allow a child to ride on the road unaccompanied. If leading on the public highway, the handler should be between the donkey and the traffic and walk on the left-hand side of the road. Reflective clothing should be worn by the handler and the rider.

Passports

It is a legal requirement that an identification passport be kept for every donkey. The donkey's passport must be available to an attending vet or a local authority enforcement officer upon request and to the Donkey Welfare Adviser in the case of donkeys in the rehoming scheme. In the event of donkeys being moved for any reason (however temporary) from the place where they are normally kept, the owners and/or transporter must ensure that the passports are available for inspection either during the journey or at the new location.

The donkey sanctuary provides all of its rehomed donkeys with passports, which must accompany the donkeys at all times during their placement.

Insurance

There are two types of insurance that you will need to consider for your donkeys: vet insurance and third party liability.

Vet Insurance

Should your donkeys become ill and need veterinary treatment, the cost can soon mount up. Complicated treatment and operations can soon add up to several thousand pounds. Talk to your vet about who they recommend and search around the different companies offering equine insurance. Make sure the insurance companies fully understand that the insurance is for a donkey, and make sure you read the small print before signing up so that you are quite clear about what is and isn't covered.

Third-Party Liability

As the caretaker of donkeys, you are responsible for any accidents that your donkeys might cause. Accidents might include a kick or a bite, or a traffic accident if your donkeys escape onto the public highway. You will need to check what restrictions there are on the policy and the extent of cover. It is also important to check you have insurance coverage if you use your donkeys at public events such as a school nativity or the local village fete. If you receive payment for using your donkeys, your donkeys might be deemed to be 'working', and you will need to ensure that you are covered for this.

Staying safe around your donkeys is of paramount importance. It is easy to become complacent with these calm, stoic creatures and take for granted their willing nature.

Here are a few tips to help you stay safe:

- Attend an introduction to donkey care courses to learn safe handling techniques.

- Always observe your donkeys' behavior before you begin work, as any changes in behavior could indicate that a donkey has a problem that might cause it to act unexpectedly or defensively.

- Always wear safe, sensible footwear when you are around donkeys. When riding or driving, always follow the recommended standard for wearing a safety hat and body protector.

- Never wrap the lead rope around your hand when handling or leading a donkey.

- Establish a good routine with your donkeys and don't change things rapidly or unexpectedly.

- In the beginning, pick up the donkeys' feet in the same way and order every time, to avoid startling them.

- Do plenty of training with your donkeys to ensure they are used to being handled, and get advice if you are uncertain or have any problems with your donkeys' behavior.

- Never walk so close behind a donkey that you could be kicked.

- Never leave a donkey unattended while it is tied up.

- Don't take your donkeys out on the road until you have done plenty of training in a safe environment.
- When you do go out on the road, be safe and be seen. Wear gloves to avoid rope burns should the donkey pull away, and high-visibility clothing so that drivers can see you.

- Remember the importance of third-party insurance.

- Never let young children handle donkeys unsupervised.

Chapter 3. Buying Your Miniature Donkey

So you have decided that you would like to own a donkey but are not sure what to look for. Have you determined what purpose you want your donkey for? Donkeys are kept as pets, for breeding, riding, harness, showing, as guardians and company for other animals. Look for and chose an animal suited to your needs. The animal control highly recommends that you purchase a female donkey (jenny) or a gelding. A male donkey (jack) is not suitable for the inexperienced owner. Donkeys need ongoing care.

Check your budget. Apart from your initial cost of purchase, there will be ongoing expenses such as regular hoof trims by a farrier, food, regular worming and veterinary costs. Donkeys are advertised for sale on the many websites, on the Internet and in classified sections of newspapers.

Whilst experienced donkey handlers do with time succeed in training the wild donkey, animal control cannot stress enough that these donkeys are not suitable for first time or inexperienced donkey owners. For the first time donkey owner, buying from a breeder that handles and trains their stock from birth or from someone who is rehoming a donkey already trained in the basics of leading, tying up and having their hooves picked up, is a much wiser choice. Although buying any livestock involves some risk, you will save yourself and the donkey heartache if you chose a donkey with the temperament and training suitable for your needs and level of experience.

From time to time there is always a donkey available for purchase, especially rescued donkeys. Although these donkeys may be in some cases less expensive than if you are buying a donkey from a breeder or owner who has stock available for sale, they are not available free of charge. Animal control sells these donkeys to recover the costs involved in their rehabilitation, training and rehoming.

First-time buyers

If you are looking to purchase your first miniature donkey, take your time, do some research and compare donkeys from farm to farm. If you do your homework, you'll have the best chance of finding the donkey that is right for you and your family, whether you are interested in a pet quality, show quality, or breeding a quality donkey. The more you know about miniature donkeys before you buy, the better for you and the donkey. If you are dealing with a reputable breeder who is genuinely concerned about the welfare of his or her animals, he or she will take the time to answer each and every question you have.

An informed, prepared new donkey owner is what we aim for when we agree to sell our donkeys to you. About 80% of our donkeys go to family homes with people who have never owned a miniature donkey before. We maintain contact with a large percentage of past customers through the years and quite often, they become our friends, not just our customers. We care about what happens to our donkeys once they leave our farm and will do our best to help you provide the best care possible by sharing our knowledge and experience.

Are you just looking for a pet?

If you are interested in owning a few donkeys as family pets, there are many options. Some people opt to go with two little boys. Geldings (castrated males) make wonderful pets. Geldings are easy to handle, make perfect, gentle pets, and are generally less expensive to purchase than jennets.

However, when purchasing a pet quality weanling jack from us, you are taking home an intact jack that was too young to be gelded prior to leaving our farm. A vet will not geld a donkey until he reaches 11-12 months of age, and even then only if they are "ready". Therefore, the responsibility and costs of gelding fall to the new owner. Costs vary but on average you should expect to pay around $200/£154 to geld a yearling jack. Pet quality jacks will be registered by us as geldings. Jack foals sold as a breeding prospect will cost more upfront than a pet quality jack and will be registered as a jack.

If you prefer owning females, jennets are just as friendly and gentle as geldings. We have had customers purchase 2 jennet foals as pets, 1 jack foal and 1 jennet foal as a pet pair, or 2 jack foals as a pet pair. Any combination works, it just depends on your personal preference. The only thing we do not encourage is keeping an intact jack as a pet. Hormones get the best of even the most gentle jack from time to time. If you are not using your boy for breeding purposes, do both him and yourself a favor and have a vet come to geld him.

Considerations before buying

With donkeys often living into their 30s, buying a donkey is a long-term commitment and a sensible, informed choice of a donkey at this early stage will ensure years of happy donkey ownership. By ensuring you find a donkey that meets your requirements and that you are able to fully meet the donkey's needs, you have the best chance of avoiding the problems and difficulties that can come with buying an unsuitable donkey.

Before proceeding to buy a donkey, ensure you have carefully considered the requirements of keeping donkeys and identified the most suitable breed, age, sex and level of handling for your situation, not just at present, but also for the upcoming years. Animal control recommends that donkeys live with other suitable donkeys and separating bonded pairs can be detrimental to the donkeys' health, so you should ensure that you will have two donkeys to keep each other company.

Checklist

The best way to avoid problems when buying a miniature donkey is to ensure you follow these steps:

- Always meet the donkey at least once before you commit to buying. Never buy "unseen" through the Internet or advertisements in papers, magazines, etc.

- Before you visit a donkey, make sure you have a very clear, written down idea of what will best suit you and your environment and what you have to offer the animal. This helps stop unsuitable emotional purchases.

- Always take another person with you to act as a witness, preferably an experienced donkey owner or consult your local donkey welfare advisor.

- When you meet the donkey, make sure you at least catch the donkey both in the stable and in a larger area, lead them around, groom and pick up all four feet.

- Make a list of questions, in advance, to ask the seller about the physical and behavioral traits of the donkeys they are selling. Ask lots of questions about the history and behavior of the animal, what training and handling they have received and health problems they have experienced.

- If you have any doubts about the behavior of the animal, ask to see the seller handle the animal and be prepared to visit them again another day before making a final decision.

- Don't let emotions cloud your judgment, which is why we recommend taking another experienced person with you. This is a long-term commitment and you want to give the right donkey the right home.

- Be prepared to walk away from donkeys that are not suitable for you and your level of experience. It is important you can give a long-term home to a donkey whose company you can safely enjoy.

- If you are buying a pedigree or miniature donkey, which could be extremely expensive, consider seeking the services of a vet to check your prospective purchase.

- Get confirmation in writing from the vendor that confirms the donkey is what they say it is.

- Passports - it is an offense to sell, buy, export, slaughter for human consumption, use for the purposes of competition or breeding any equine that does not have a passport. The passport should remain with the animal for its lifetime.

Buying from a dealer

The Sale of Goods Act applies only if you buy an equine from a person classified as a 'dealer'. Buying from a dealer can offer the best protection.

If you find your donkey has a problem, making him unsuitable for the purpose you bought him, you're entitled to your money back – even if the dealer denies knowledge.

Reputable dealers will agree in writing to take a donkey back if it has a physical or behavioral problem and either refund the purchase price or offer an exchange. Don't let the dealer take the donkey back to sell it on your behalf. You, and not the dealer, could be sued by the next owner if you fail to disclose a problem.

If there's a problem, act straight away. The longer you leave it, the more you risk losing your right to a full refund, although you'll still be able to claim damages.

The Sale Of Goods Act implies certain conditions of sale; your 'Statutory Rights' are:

- The donkey must be of reasonable or satisfactory quality – for instance, free of defects such as lameness unless you have prior knowledge and accept the condition. The donkey must be fit for the purpose for which it was generally sold, or any purpose made known at the time of the agreement.

- He must be 'as described'. If your new eight-year-old turns out to be one, it's a breach of trading standards.

- If one or all of these criteria are not met, you may be entitled to a full refund or the difference in value between the donkey you thought you were buying and the one you got.

Buying Privately

Buying privately is a different matter. The law 'caveat emptor' (let the buyer beware) exists. If the donkey has a problem, you must be able to prove the seller knew, or ought to have known, about it in order for you to get a refund.

Suing for breach of contract can be difficult, lengthy and costly. It is very important to follow the checklist above to minimize the risk of buying a suitable donkey.

Selecting your donkeys

Points to consider before purchase:

- Why do you want donkeys? Donkeys are wanted for many reasons, as pets or companion animals, for riding or driving, for showing, working on smallholdings or for breeding purposes.

- Do you have the time and commitment needed to look after them? It will take at least an hour a day to provide care for your donkeys and their environment.

- Do you have approximately half an acre (2000 square meters) of suitable and safe grazing and/or turn out land for each donkey, with a shelter with hard standing, a fresh water supply, and electricity?

- Do you have a vet, farrier and equine dental technician who understands donkeys and is prepared to undertake their routine treatments?

- Do you have a supplier of hay and straw?

- Do you have storage space for hay and straw over the winter months? Hay and straw can be cheaper if you can buy in bulk before the winter.

- Can you remove your muck heap regularly? Is there a local farmer who will take it away?

- Can you afford the cost of caring for a donkey? We give a general average guide of $1300/£1000 per donkey per year.

- You should also be aware of the need to maintain adequate contingency funds to meet unexpected veterinary bills or take out insurance that covers such costs, and we would advise the need for third-party insurance.

The likely costs

You will need a good shelter and adequate fencing in place beforehand and will need to factor in the cost of feed (hay and straw), bedding, worming, vets' fees and regular farrier visits, which all vary according to the health and age of your donkeys.

Prices on donkeys vary greatly depending on the region of the country and the quality of the animal. Pet jacks are the most economical in the $200/£154 to $600/£462 range.
The next step up would be a breeder quality jack, weanling or adult, any color, and friendly with nice conformation and will run in the neighborhood of $700/£539 to $1200/£923. Top quality jacks and jennets can run upwards from there.

What buyers should expect

- Animals to be in good physical condition whether to be sold as a pet or as breeding stock.

- To be provided health and breeding history with full disclosure of any pertinent information the owner should be aware of.

- Animals to be behaviorally sound, living within the herd and not weaned earlier than 4 - 6 months of age.

- Registration certificate, signed transfer, and pedigree records current with the registry of choice.

- Any sales guarantees should be spelled out and signed.
- Breeding stock that represent the guidelines outlined in the Miniature Donkey Breed Standard.

- Information about the breed with care, diet and other necessary information provided.

- The newly purchased donkey to be up to date on vaccinations, worming and hoof trimming. This information should be in writing with dates and types of vaccines.

- A properly-fitted halter and lead included in the sale.

Buyers should seek out breeders who adhere to the above principles and thereby demonstrate their responsibilities to both the buyer and the breed.

Breeder responsibilities

Reputable miniature donkey breeders have the responsibility to:

- Breed their donkeys with the future of the miniature donkey gene pool foremost in mind using the guidelines outlined in the Miniature Donkey Breed Standard.

- Select breeding pairs with the intention of improving the offspring.

- Promote the breed honestly to people who are interested and discourage people from buying on impulse or those who cannot adequately provide for them.

- Avoid breeding solely for short-term market fads such as size or color.

- Maintain current health and registry records.

- Be honest in sales and advertising - offer animals that are realistically priced reflecting their conformation, sex, age, and health conditions.

- Follow up with buyers to assure that they are satisfied with their animals and that the donkeys are properly cared for.

- Provide proper shelter and diet for their miniature donkeys.

- Breed jennets only when they are physically and mentally mature - three years and older.

- Breed no smaller than the recommended minimum height (over 30" at the withers) as stated in the Breed Standard.

- Continue to breed only if there is a market for the offspring and if the animals will make a contribution to the breed.

- Register or transfer all donkeys before they leave the farm.
- Geld the majority of jack foals.

- Be prepared to humanely euthanize donkeys that are old, ill, or unable to be placed in a caring home.

Responsible breeders who base their actions on the ethical principles set out above build solid reputations, serve as role models for future breeders and contribute to the integrity of the miniature donkey breed.

Chapter 4. General Care

Donkeys come from Africa and have only been in the US and other parts of Europe for a few hundred years - not long enough for them to adapt to the wet climate. Donkeys do not have waterproof coats, therefore shelter is absolutely essential for their comfort and well-being.

This can be a simple construction but should have a roof and preferably three and a half sides, facing away from the prevailing wind. The floor should be dry, bedded with straw or wood shavings and cleaned out regularly to prevent the build-up of bacteria in the manure, which attack the donkeys' hooves, causing foot problems.

If you know horses you already know how to care for a donkey. Treat him like a small, quiet natured horse and things will go smoothly. However, there are a few special concerns about donkey care that are worth noting.

There is so much to learn about donkeys and their kin, so much to do with them, and so much pure enjoyment of them as individual "people with long ears", that donkey owners never seem to get tired of them. So if you are an equine fan, try a donkey, you won't regret it!

Shelter

Miniature donkeys need shelter in a barn or a 3-sided shelter in order to be able to get in from rain, wind, snow and even extreme sunshine in the summer months. They cannot survive without shelter of some sort. Winter care is more about helping your donkeys withstand the lower temperatures and stay healthy in the cold or wet weather, rather than shutting them in completely. Providing that your donkeys have constant access to adequate shelter, most donkeys will prefer the freedom of being out even in the colder weather as opposed to being shut in a stable for days on end.

From a donkey's point of view, his worst possible scenario during the winter is not a cold and frosty day, but a day which is both wet and windy. Although your field may have some natural shelter such as trees and hedgerows, due to the donkeys lack of waterproof coat, a proper shelter is really imperative for your once desert-dwelling animal to enjoy a comfortable winter and any season for that matter.

A suitable donkey shelter should be a structure of least three sides and a sloping roof, sited in a sheltered area, and preferably with a concrete base. The shelter should have solid walls from the ground up, be free from draughts and be waterproof. It is important when choosing a location for your shelter that the opening side is out of prevailing winds. The floor of the shelter will need to be covered with fresh bedding. A fenced area of hard standing next to your shelter or stable is a necessary requirement for your donkey should he need to be shut off the wet, muddy, or frosty ground for a period of time.

Hooves

Donkey feet are incredibly tough yet pliable and will not under normal domestic circumstances wear down or chip off like horse's hooves do. You will have to keep your donkey's feet properly trimmed, or he may develop "Sultan's slipper" feet.

Donkey's hooves grow very fast and should be trimmed by a qualified, registered professional every 8 to 10 weeks. This costs between $15/12-$25/£19 depending on the farrier and how far they have had to travel to get to you. In their natural environment, donkeys will travel up to 20 miles a day browsing for food.

The terrain would be mostly sand, shale and rocks, so the hooves are designed to grow quickly to combat the inevitable wearing down. When we put them on soft land with rich grass, they very quickly suffer from long and distorted hooves and laminitis, a painful condition due to overfeeding and/or stress (from traveling, losing a friend, moving premises, etc).

Their hooves should be cleaned out with a hoof pick every day if possible but certainly a couple of times a week to remove small stones and sharp chippings, which may become lodged in the hoof and cause lameness. Never use a nail or other sharp instrument to clean the hooves, as it is surprisingly easy to puncture the sole or even damage the hoof wall. Bacteria will die when exposed to air, but should you want to insure that your donkey's feet are perfectly clean, you can squirt a solution of 1 part Clorox to 4 parts water onto the sole of the hoof. Be careful to not squirt it on any area that has hair, as it could cause irritation.

Donkeys are herd animals

As stated before, it is unnatural and unkind to keep them on their own. Donkeys crave company, especially of their own kind, though they may be companioned by a horse, pony or even, in some cases, cattle or goats… but they generally much prefer another donkey. They are highly social animals with a sophisticated hierarchy within the herd. The herd may 'belong' to a stallion but is organized by a 'lead mare' who makes most of the decisions. Stallions kept on their own are often noisy, as they bray constantly for a mate.

Grooming

Most donkeys love to be groomed, especially in the late spring and early summer when they lose their heavy winter coats. This can take several weeks and they are generally just looking smart again when it is time to grow a new winter coat. Any of the brushes used for horse grooming are suitable - dandy brush, body brush with a curry comb to clean it, or plastic curry comb. Dog slicker brushes are also very useful provided you do not lean on them too hard and scratch the skin. Simply remove all the dry dirt and brush lightly and consistently the way the hair lies but be careful under the belly. The donkey may be ticklish and will kick to tell you so! Wash the areas around eyes, nostrils and dock with lukewarm water using a separate soft sponge for each area. It is natural for a donkey's eyes to water and form little crusty bits - these can simply be rubbed off gently. Never groom your donkey when he is wet.

Your donkey can be brushed and bathed although there is nothing better to a donkey after a good bath than a good roll in the dirt. A good dust bath keeps flies off. There are many equine shampoos on the market, and you can find grooming brushes at most feed stores and mail order catalogs.
We like to trim our donkeys' manes close to their necks in the summertime. It also makes them look groomed and cared for. Donkeys can also be body clipped to remove winter shaggy hair. Body clipping makes it cooler for them in the summer, but exposes the skin to flies. In addition, spotted donkeys are more susceptible to

sunburn when body clipped. Do not body clip late in the year, as it takes several months to grow out and winter winds may arrive before your donkey's winter coat does. Brushing in the spring will help to remove the longer hair of winter.

Rugs

They are available to fit donkeys - both stable rugs and weatherproof, New Zealand outdoor rugs. For a young, healthy donkey with good shelter, these would not normally be necessary, but they are invaluable for sick or older donkeys or as a temporary measure if you have inadequate shelter.

Teeth

Some donkeys, particularly older ones, need their teeth rasping occasionally by a vet, a qualified farrier or a qualified equine dentist. As their teeth wear through chewing, sharp spurs can form along the edges of the molars, which make it painful for the donkey to eat. Weight loss in an otherwise healthy donkey and little 'quids' of half-chewed food spat out on the floor are both indications of possible tooth trouble. The donkey does not have the same nerves in his teeth that we do, so rasping when carried out correctly is not painful.

Tack

A good quality collar or halter will be needed for holding the donkey when the farrier or vet is tending to him and for moving from one place to another. Never leave a halter or collar on the donkey permanently, as it may rub, get caught up on something or, on a young donkey, refuse to grow when he does. Donkeys are affectionate and greedy and therefore very easily bribed to come to you and to follow instructions. Even a very timid donkey will soon gain confidence when he is offered tidbits (carrots, apples, brown bread, mints and ginger biscuits) and petted regularly without necessarily having something done to him - but beware of overfeeding or encouraging him to bite by teasing with tidbits. Full riding and driving tackle for donkeys is available through some saddlers, but is not as easily available as a tack for ponies and horses.

Transporting Donkeys

Optimal Welfare Standards

Current legislations have strict transport guidelines relating to the movement of all commercial livestock. These restrictions do not yet apply to private animals but they may in the future. These recommendations are worth following in all situations to ensure optimal welfare standards are maintained. If you are traveling abroad please ensure you check with your vet with regard to health certificates.

Tips

If you are loading/traveling with donkeys for the first time or are not familiar with them then leave plenty of time for loading. Better still, if it is not an emergency, schedule a practice run beforehand. If this does not go smoothly, practice daily and maybe feed the donkey in the trailer each time. Make the box and entrance as inviting as possible. Park the trailer carefully to block the escape route from the sides and reduce the ramp height. It is recommended to go for a short drive if the first journey planned is a long one. The driver must be competent at towing before driving with an animal on board.

Transport Recommendations

All journeys made using the basic trailer towed behind a vehicle should not exceed a journey time of 8 hours. If borrowing a trailer always thoroughly check the floor, lights, ramp and catches for safety.

Check the towing capacity of the vehicle with the manufacturer. Ensure the trailer complies with the legal requirements for road use e.g. tires, brake cables, registration plate and spare wheel.

A specially-designed lorry is required for journeys exceeding 8 hours, or those including a ferry or train journey. Sufficient space, ventilation, food and water must be provided.

A lot of energy is used in maintaining balance whilst traveling. Careful driving can greatly reduce stress to the donkey(s). Attention must be paid to ensure slow acceleration, braking and cornering.

Choose the route most suited to ensure a smooth, continuous journey.

Plan the journey carefully to avoid traffic delays, as the ventilation within the box normally depends on forward movement. Have a map in case you need to look up an alternative route and avoid traveling during the heat of the day during the summer.

Bedding within a trailer or horsebox should be sufficient to absorb urine and feces for the entire journey unless frequently cleaned out.

It is ideal to have rubber matting and minimal bedding for comfort and support; ideally dust extracted bedding such as shavings. A reduction in the amount of bedding improves the air quality within the box.

Ensure you leave the box clean after use and ready for the next journey. Do not carry spare filled hay nets on the outside of the vehicle/trailer, as the hay or haylage will absorb pollutants from vehicle emissions.

Carry a mobile phone, fully charged and with relevant telephone numbers on it i.e. vet, relative, destination contact, breakdown recovery, etc.

If possible, take someone who is used to the donkeys with you. Carry drinking water and buckets, (in the towing vehicle not the trailer). Take the donkeys' passports with you in case you are stopped by the police or need to call a vet.

Take at least one spare head collar and lead rope and carry a torch and first aid kit for personal use and a fluorescent waist coat. Furthermore, ensure the vehicle is adequate fuelled before you set off.

It is worth noting that most stress occurs at loading and unloading. Plan both stages to minimize stress by having experienced helpers, ideally familiar with the donkey. It is best to take a supply of damp hay or haylage if the journey is a long one, or involves a rest stop. Some individuals will not eat whilst traveling but the option must be available. Hay should ideally be fed from the floor to reduce the risk of entrapment in hay nets.

As donkeys can bond extremely strongly to other donkeys as well as other animals, it is very important to ensure any bonded companion animals travel as well. Failure to do so could result in extreme stress to the animals involved.

Check the animals on board at the start of the journey for signs of distress.
The animals should be checked and offered water every 4 hours.

Toys

Donkeys are much more cerebral than horses and can be destructive when bored. Toys will help with this and watching donkeys play is an absolute delight for their people. Donkeys love hula hoops, beach balls, corrugated drain pipe rings, cardboard boxes with no staples, feed pans, hoses with the ends cut off, etc. The list is endless and fun. They also love hills of any kind and in my pastures we have added piles of dirt just for the donkeys to play on. Donkeys also love piles of shavings and piles of sand. They will push the shavings around with their noses, paw in it, and roll with exuberance.

Chapter 5. Feeding Your Miniature Donkey

The basic necessities of clean, fresh water, trace mineral salt, and a source of dietary fiber and calories in the form of hay or pasture apply to donkeys. Protein requirements of full-size equines may be safely applied. The specific nutritional requirements of donkeys have not been established. It is reasonable to apply horse data to donkeys, but the donkey's feral origin has adapted them to subsistence on low-quality forages. The donkey is a monogastric herbivore that eats roughage, such as straw and hay, and is able to utilize cellulose and hemicelluloses from plants very efficiently.

Donkeys are capable of digesting and processing low-quality feed compared to horses. Their digestive systems adapted to arid areas with poor grazing, as in Africa and Asia. Donkeys are termed "trickle feeders" and evolved to have fiber passing almost continuously through their gastrointestinal tract. Consequently, when they are fed similar high-quality and high-calorie feed as given to horses, they become overweight and subjected to nutritional-excess problems, such as obesity, laminitis, and hepatic (fatty liver) disease.

Donkeys need more fiber and less protein in their diets than horses. They are not ruminants so must not be fed like cattle, sheep, or goats. Donkeys with access to cattle licks containing urea should be restricted in their intake to avoid urea poisoning. Donkeys generally are more selective than horses in their food consumption, using their relatively narrow muzzles and mobile lips to sort through feed material.

Like horses, they spend a great deal of time eating when turned out on pasture in favorable environmental conditions. Donkeys prefer shelter to rain and will remain inside when possible to avoid insects. They may search pastures for the most appealing plants if allowed free access to large areas, resulting in inefficient pasture use; rotational strip grazing is a more efficient method of pasture management. If feeding time is restricted in working donkeys, they may resort to fast, incomplete chewing of forages, leading to digestive problems such as esophageal choke (obstruction) or intestinal impaction.

The amount needed depends on climatic conditions and on individual metabolism. Donkeys in northern climates with wintry conditions need more calories than in warmer months to offset the energy expenditure required to maintain body temperature. A limited amount of moderate quality hay and/or free choice, poorer quality pasture or hay may suffice for donkeys in warmer climates.

It is important to regularly assess the body condition of each individual donkey to ensure that he is neither overweight nor too thin; the diet should be adjusted accordingly. It is equally important to ensure that all animals have equal access to food. If pastures are overgrazed due to overcrowding or if animals are kept in close proximity to larger or more aggressive animals, they will not be able to consume enough calories and may suffer serious weight loss and starvation. This is especially critical for winter time feeding in northern climates.

A study conducted by the University of Edinburgh and University of Central Mexico determined the maintenance requirements for fit, healthy donkeys. Results showed that donkeys require 1.3% to 1.7% of their body weight in forage daily, depending on the season; the lower value applies to summer. For maintenance, they needed 88 to 117 kJ DE (digestible energy)/kg of body weight), with the lower value corresponding to summer. In practical terms, this means that a donkey requires feedstuffs with low energy values so he can eat large enough quantities to satisfy a natural appetite without becoming obese.

Water

Your donkey should have access to good, clean water 24 hours a day at all times. You may find it easier to install a float valve on your trough. Troughs should be cleaned when needed, especially in the summer when the heat can cause bacteria and algae to grow faster than in winter. Caution should be taken when foals are around troughs. Do not use a trough so low to the ground that a foal could fall in and drown.

Supplemental Feeding

If you ask 10 donkey owners or breeders their views on supplemental feeding, you will get 10 different responses and all will, in all probability, work very well for their animals. The key is to observe how your graining (supplemental feeding) is affecting your donkey's body condition. There are several types of supplemental feeds. One grain that is used frequently is crimped oats (must be "crimped" oats, not whole oats). Crimped oats are usually 10% protein with some crude fat. Donkeys do well with this grain because it's in a pure form. A second grain that's widely used is called horse and mule feed or sweet feed. This feed comes in 10, 12, and 14 percent protein amounts. We stopped using horse and mule feed for our mature donkeys because we found that it was putting weight on our donkeys but not muscle, probably because it contains "sweet" additives such as molasses. Another feed is regular horse pellets that you can get in 10, 12, and 14 percent protein amounts.

These feeds can be used for your lactating jennets (females that are nursing foals) and for foals and yearlings. The third type of supplemental feed comes in various brand names but is commonly referred to as a total or balanced nutritional supplement. Products such as Strategy, Omaline 100, 200, and 300 are examples of this feed, all by Purina. These products contain protein, but also contain a good balance of vitamins and minerals. Although more expensive than other supplements, these are a complete nutritional package for your donkey. We feed Omaline 200 to our show donkeys, our weanlings, and any donkey in need of weight gain. We find that it gets the youngsters off to a good nutritional start.

With crimped oats, we suggest feeding no more than a 1lb. coffee can full per feeding, preferably 1/2 a coffee can full. With horse and mule feed, the amount should be reduced. With your total nutritional supplements, follow the recommended amounts on the bag. We feed a coffee can or half a coffee can per feeding depending on the age and size of the donkey and whether or not they are prone to being overweight, in which case we cut the supplemental feed way back. As with all feed, you need to monitor the effectiveness of your feeding program, then adjust the amount being fed, the frequency of your feeding, type of feed you are offering, or eliminate supplemental feed completely depending on your donkey's body condition. Just remember, foals, yearlings, and nursing jennies require more protein and supplemental feeding than do mature donkeys.

Never feed more than 14% protein. In addition, do not let your pregnant jennet become fat because that can complicate a pregnancy and delivery. That's why we either eliminate completely or reduce the amount of supplemental feed during the last trimester of pregnancy. The foal is already developed and too much feed will just add weight and size to the foal, thereby increasing the risk of complications at birth. Historically, miniature donkeys are used to sparse food supplies that were native in their ancestral homes of Sicily and Sardinia. Don't over feed your donkey. You will find them developing a fat roll or crest on the top of their necks, which does not go away if they are eating too much or too rich a diet. If this happens, cut down the supplemental feed by amount, protein percentage, frequency, or eliminate entirely.

Sweet feeds and high protein feeds encourage milk production, which is good for the lactating jennet, but a note of caution is appropriate here regarding mom and the new foal. I don't give any feed to a new mom for the first week after giving birth unless she is not producing a good supply of milk, in which case, giving her feed will encourage milk production. If given too much supplemental feed after delivery, her bag may become too large and the baby may not be able to keep up with production. In some cases, that can create mastitis, which causes inflammation and an infection of the udder and must be treated with antibiotics.

Take a look at her bag after delivery and if you feel you must feed her, give her very small amounts to begin with and increase the amount over time. It will not hurt her or the foal to be without supplemental feed until the baby is nursing well. Conversely, the feed can help stimulate milk production to the under producing jennet, so you can begin feeding her after delivery but in small amounts. Always look at the nipples to make sure the foal is nursing both sides. They should be pliable and not engorged if the foal is nursing properly.

Minerals

A trace mineral supplement such as 12-12 should be made available to your donkeys at all times. They will eat it as needed. When purchasing your minerals, be sure it is recommended for equines. 12-12 minerals for equine are a different product than 12-12 minerals for cattle. Cattle products can contain urea, which is toxic to donkeys. We use a product called Purina Horse Minerals, which comes in granular form rather than the hard mineral blocks, although we keep the blocks out for them as well. We think it is easier for the donkey, especially foals, to eat the granular minerals. Since a donkey does not have all of its permanent teeth until age five, they may not be able to use the block very well if teeth are missing. A salt block may also be made available to them.

We always make sure we feed our donkeys with the right foods to ensure they stay healthy. Donkey nutrition varies from animal to animal depending on their age and health requirements. In their natural habitat donkeys will browse, eating highly fibrous plant material in small quantities throughout the day. During the spring and summer, the donkeys at the donkey sanctuary have access to restricted grazing. In addition to the restricted grazing, our donkeys always have access to barley straw to ensure they are getting plenty of fiber to meet their nutritional needs. The amount of grass donkeys have access to is controlled; either by strip grazing using electric fencing or by co-grazing with other species to prevent them from becoming overweight.

During the winter months, the donkeys are housed in large airy barns with concrete run-out yards, without access to grass. Instead, our donkeys have access to barley straw and are fed a controlled amount of hay or haylage according to their body condition. In special circumstances, old or sick donkeys eat additional high fiber feeds and supplements to help maintain their body weight.

Straw

We recommend feeding donkeys quality barley straw, as it is high in fiber and low in sugar, and closely resembles the food that a donkey would eat in the wild. Constant access to straw will allow a donkey to eat to appetite without consuming too many calories. Too many additional calories and there is a risk the donkey could put on excess weight, which has associated risks of developing health conditions such as laminitis and hyperlipaemia. Oat straw may be useful for old or underweight donkeys, as this usually has a slightly higher nutritional value than barley straw. Wheat straw is very fibrous and has lower energy values, but may be fed to young healthy donkeys with a good set of teeth. Linseed straw is best avoided since the seed is poisonous to donkeys unless it has been boiled, and it is very difficult to ensure that no seed is present in the straw. If straw is in short supply then priority must be given to using it as a feed source and alternative bedding such as shavings should be used.

Hay

Good quality horse hay should be fed to your donkey in the winter or if your donkey is in a dry lot, meaning there is little to no grass available. If your pasture is rich and of a good quality grass such as coastal Bermuda (in Texas, for example), hay isn't necessary during the summer. If your pasture does not have grass, you will need to feed hay. In addition, if you find your donkey getting fat after it has reached maturity, discontinue or reduce its intake of hay and/or grain while on pasture, but only in summer months. Hay should be given at all times during the winter when pasture is unavailable. Hay bales of coastal Bermuda or another quality hay native to your region are preferred over alfalfa because alfalfa hay is too rich in protein. Many owners feed hay twice a day if the pasture is sparse or if the donkey is in a dry lot.

Feeding twice daily will control your donkey's diet, keep him trim, and permit you to observe your donkey frequently for illness or injury. Twice a day feeding is, of course, more labor intensive but has its merits. Because of the number of donkeys at Quarter Moon Ranch, we free feed in the winter, meaning we leave hay out continually so that they may eat at will. We carefully observe our donkeys to make sure they are not getting too fat or too thin, in which case we will adjust their feeding and/or supplemental feed program. Show donkeys are taken off pasture or free fed hay to avoid their getting grass or hay bellies prior to a show.

If you plan to feed your donkeys hay during the winter months, ensure you have enough forage in store to see you through the winter, as supplies could run out before the winter is over. Never feed donkeys moldy hay, as they may have potentially fatal allergies to the mold. It is best to try and build up a good relationship with your hay supplier to make sure you have a consistent supply of good, clean hay suitable for feeding to your donkeys.

Different types of hay available include:

- Meadow Hay: This is a natural mix of grasses made from grass grown on old pasture and is suitable for feeding to donkeys.

- Seed Hay: This is also good for donkeys. It is a planted crop of specific grasses, such as rye or timothy; which the farmer makes from the stems remaining after the grain has been taken.

- Hay produced from cow pasture: This will usually have higher energy levels and may be less suitable if fed on its own. However, it could be fed mixed with a higher ratio of straw.

- Ragwort in hay is very poisonous to donkeys, but unfortunately, it can be quite hard to distinguish once it has dried, this is why it is important to know and trust your hay supplier.

Weather conditions tend to influence the cutting season - late May to July. Remember, late cut hay will have lower energy values, which may suit your donkeys if they are overweight and require forage with a lower energy content, but not if they are elderly/underweight donkeys that need feeding up. If the hay is cut later in the year a lot of the goodness will have gone out of the grass and some of the grass will have gone to seed. This type of hay provides a much lower energy source than early cut hay and for that reason, it is fine for feeding to donkeys. If the weather in May is good, the farmers might make hay in the first week of June and get a second cut at the end of

July. This 'second cut' hay is usually lower in energy value and again is fine for most donkeys.

Freshly cut hay should be stored in a dry barn for at least three months before feeding. Do not suddenly introduce freshly cut hay to the donkey's diet, as it could cause colic or laminitis. Reduce the risk by mixing the new hay with the previous year's hay, or mix it with straw over a few days so there is a gradual change over. If hay is in short supply in your area (or if it is very expensive) then you could look at the following alternatives.

Haylage is semi-wilted grass that has been allowed to dry to only 55-65% dry matter (as compared to 85% in hay). The grass is baled, compressed and sealed in tough plastic and the resultant forage is virtually dust-free, highly palatable and nutritious. Once the plastic wrapping is broken (deliberately or accidentally) fungal spores start to grow so the haylage must be used within three to four days (less in warm weather) or discarded. This is why it is better suited to those with more than one or two donkeys to feed. If there are any signs of mold or yeast growth on a bale once opened, it should be discarded, as should any uneaten haylage as this could be toxic to the donkeys.

Haylage can be very variable in terms of nutritional levels; some haylage may be too high in energy to feed to donkeys. If you are unsure about the suitability of locally available haylage as donkey food, we would recommend having it analyzed (most of the large horse feed companies provide this service for a small fee) or feeding a commercially available equine haylage marketed as 'laminitis safe'.

Silage

Silage is not suitable for feeding to donkeys because the moisture level is usually too high, with a low pH, and a low fiber and high protein level.

High fiber cubes

There are many brands on the market selling high fiber cubes. Products marketed for equines prone to laminitis are a good choice because they are usually high in fiber and low in sugar. High fiber cubes are a good choice if you need more than grass, hay and straw to build up the weight of an old or underweight donkey. Care must be taken that the donkey does not eat the cubes too quickly, as it may cause colic, so add water and mix with a small quantity of low sugar chaff when introducing cubes for the first time. High fiber cubes can be soaked down to a mash: particularly useful for donkeys with poor teeth. Avoid any cubes containing cereal,s as these are not suitable for feeding to donkeys. Products marketed as 'mixes' are usually cereal based and again not suitable.

Short chop chaff products

Consider feeding your donkey chaff, a mixture of chopped up hay and/or straw. There are many types of chaff on the market. These contain variable amounts of chopped rye, timothy or alfalfa grasses and oat straw. Some have added oil, molasses, minerals, herbs or hoof growth supplements, whilst others are high fiber and molasses free. Chaff products marketed for equines prone to laminitis are good for donkeys that have difficulty eating grass, hay and straw due to poor dentition, and can be used as feed supplements or fed ad lib as a total hay/straw replacer. Always choose a chaff which is 'laminitis safe' and preferably with a sugar content of less than 8% when feeding donkeys.

Dried sugar beet pulp

Sugar beet is a useful food given in small amounts to tempt a sick donkey to eat. Sugar beet is a source of succulent, nutritious, digestible fiber when added to the feed, although it cannot be fed as a replacement to hay. We recommend unmolassed sugar beet to avoid laminitis. Dried sugar beet pulp is available in shredded or cubed form and must be thoroughly soaked before feeding and used within 24 hours once wet. Soaking times vary so refer to the manufacturer's instructions. There are now some quick-soak, unmolassed sugar beet products on the market ,which soak in less than ten minutes, although it's always advisable to check the product is fully soaked before giving them to your donkeys.

Succulents

Fruit and vegetables can be fed in small amounts (one or two a day) to provide variety and encourage a healthy appetite. They are a worthwhile addition to the normal food ration in winter and early spring when fresh grass is not available. Avoid feeding potatoes, anything from the brassica family, onions, leeks, garlic, stoned fruit and anything which is old, fermented or moldy as these are toxic to donkeys.

Carrots, apples, bananas, pears, turnips and swedes are all safe and usually very popular with donkeys. Ensure that chopped fruit and vegetables are cut in a way that minimizes the risk of choking, such as in sticks.

Minerals and Vitamins

Donkeys usually obtain all of the required vitamins and minerals from the straw, grass and hay in their diets. However, we recommend that in addition to the standard food you supply that they have free access to an equine mineralized block, which contains various minerals including salt, to supplement their diet all year round to prevent any deficiencies. Blocks designed for other livestock may be toxic to donkeys as some contain inappropriate mineral levels.

General Considerations

- All feed should be of high quality.

- All equines are sensitive to toxins that can be found in spoiled feeds.

- All feed should be free from mold.

- All changes to their diet should be made gradually, over at least 7-14 days.

- Donkeys prefer to browse for their bulk and fiber throughout the day.

- Donkeys prefer to eat little and often. Provide ad lib barley straw.

- Do not over feed your donkey; check the body condition of your donkey regularly.

- Donkeys do not need high levels of sugar in their diets.

If in any doubt about the energy value or the quality of any feed, it is advisable to seek expert advice.

Always provide a mineral lick and permanent access to a clean water supply.

Never feed grass clippings and ensure that your neighbors are aware of the dangers of doing this, as it can lead to colic.

Toxic Plants

There are a few plants that are toxic to all equine. Consult your vet and/or county agent for those that you may have in your area and seek their advice on the subject. Mesquite pods are probably more toxic than most. Do not panic if you have any toxic plants in your pasture. If you are feeding properly, your donkeys will have no need of eating a plant that is toxic. If your donkeys are eating an abundance of acorns in the fall, you may want to give them small amounts of wheat bran to flush the bowels out during acorn season, as those can be a problem. Once again, consult your veterinarian to help with your health care program.

Thoughtless disposal of garden rubbish, such as hedge trimmings containing yew or privet, etc. is the most common cause of sporadic cases of poisoning. Let your well-meaning neighbors know that any garden waste such as hedge clippings or grass cuttings are potentially fatal, and should never be put in the paddock.

If you take your donkeys for walks or to events, make sure they cannot access poisonous plants. For instance, yew is one of the most toxic plants and is commonly found in church yards, so if your donkey is attending a Christmas Nativity they may attempt to snatch a bite. Some trees are quite safe for most of the year but need to be fenced off during the fruiting season. This includes all fruit trees, beech and oak trees.

Curiosity and boredom are key factors in the eating of unsavory foliage and plant matter; good fencing and the provision of safe boredom breakers such as bramble, gorse or herb patches or cut branches from hazel, ash, hawthorn, apple, limited willow, alder, lime and poplar trees.

Common Ragwort

Ragwort is a yellow flowering weed and is poisonous both dead and alive.

Ragwort is frequently seen on wasteland, verges and railway land whereby it spreads onto pasture land. It normally takes two years to grow to maturity and then flowers biennially (every second year).

However, if the stem is cut or mown, ragwort often becomes an annual flowering plant. Each plant can produce up to 150,000 seeds which have a 70% germination rate and can lie dormant in the soil for up to 20 years.

Be very aware of this weed both on your pasture and in the hay. Ragwort can cause serious liver damage over a period of time. Ragwort must be pulled with gloves and burnt. It should never be composted. Pull the plant up before it flowers to avoid spreading seeds.

Horsetail (Mare's Tail)

All varieties are poisonous but common horsetail and marsh horsetail are most likely to cause poisoning.

It is a perennial plant with a creeping underground stem from which green, jointed, upright stems grow in spring. Control of mare's tail is extremely difficult, if you experience this plant on your land we would advise talking to an agricultural specialist about available control methods. Poisoning is most likely to occur when horsetail is present in hay or bedding.

Bracken

Bracken is a common fern that grows throughout Britain and you must be careful it does not dominate your grassland. The whole plant contains several toxic substances, some of which remain after cutting and drying.

Donkeys may develop a taste for bracken when other forage is in poor supply. Poisoning tends to be cumulative over a period of time.

Rhododendron

An evergreen shrub with tough and leathery elongated leaves, dark green above and paler beneath. The large, cone-shaped buds develop into domed clusters of bell-shaped flowers. Rhododendrons are often eaten when animals escape and eat the garden hedgerow or garden clippings or when food is scarce. Can kill after a few hours of being eaten.

Chapter 6. Training Your Miniature Donkey

Training your donkey is really not much different from training horses and mules, though there are differences in instinct and attitude that will determine your approach in given situations. The mechanics and techniques, however, remain the same.

The donkey foal needs to begin his life of training with imprinting. Imprinting is simply getting your donkey accustomed to your touch, your voice, your smell, the way you look, and the way you interact with him. These are all the things he learns from his mother that will determine the design of his character as he grows older.

If he is to be a trainable and tractable individual, you and his mother must teach him to be accepting and willing from the day he is born. This also implies that you and the mother cannot be at odds. She needs to possess the traits you wish to instill in the foal.

A well-trained mother will help to produce a well-trained foal. If your jennet is not easy to handle, then she needs this training as well, and should be started with imprinting and progress through the steps of training before the foal is born.

When imprinting the foal, think of the kind of attitude you want to cultivate in him. Do not come at him with the idea that he must accept you. This is a forceful and intrusive attitude and can foster resistance.

Come at him with love, patience and kindness and these are the things he will learn. Give him respect and ask that he respect you and he will begin to learn about behavioral limitations. If he were in a herd, the adults would demand that he respect their space with well-placed discipline. You must learn to do the same without overdoing it. If he bites or kicks, a well-placed tap on the side of the mouth or rump will do the trick.

Rewarding his good behavior consistently will reinforce repetition of what you desire from him and will foster understanding between you both. This is the beginning of a long lasting bond of friendship. Friendships would not be complete without a good balance of work and play.

Teachers who make learning fun for children make it easier for the child to learn what he or she needs to and encourage a good attitude towards life in general that can carry them through the most trying of situations. The donkey is no different. If learning is fun and non-threatening, he will enjoy his time with you and you will discover his innate desire to please and to serve.

The best teachers are those who realize that they too can learn from the child in this process. Each individual is different in their own way and it is important to recognize the difference in order to foster confidence and self-assurance.

The donkey will appreciate that you not only wish to teach him, but to learn from him as well. This will encourage his enthusiasm for learning and will assure that he learns well and confidently. He will learn, right from the beginning, to want to follow you anywhere – because it's the best place to be!

Don't rush your donkey. Horses have a very quick response time as a rule, with minimal comprehension and memory retention. A donkey's response time is measurably slower (they appear to be in deep thought for what seems like an eternity to you or me), but their comprehension and memory retention is the keenest. When training each of these different equines, you need to learn to gauge your body language and expectations accordingly.

Whether your donkey is a young foal or an older animal, begin with imprinting and do the steps in sequence. Learn how to put on the halter properly, let him wear it for awhile, then take it off, as he could get caught and injure himself. When he is not bothered by you putting on and taking off the halter, you can teach him to be tied. Put on the halter and tie him to a safe post. Come by to see him every ten or fifteen minutes, untie him and ask him to "come". If he does not take a step towards you, just retie him and leave.

Come back in ten minutes and try again. When he takes a step towards you, reward him with a treat and lots of praise. Stroke him on the neck and shoulder, on the poll between the ears or scratch his chest or rump...whichever he finds most pleasing. Then try a few more steps.

Don't ask for any more steps each day than he is willing to give. Save them for the next time and soon he will lead easily. When he is leading easily, you can start taking walks around the farm and begin to introduce him to things he may find frightening. Lead him as close as he will go at your shoulder, then step towards the obstacle as close as the lead will allow and coax him to you. Offer a reward if necessary to entice him and be sure to reward him when he comes forward. When he is confident about investigating things with you, you can progress to an obstacle course.

At first try over logs, a bridge, tires, or other such obstacles. You may find your donkey reluctant to pick up his feet to negotiate an obstacle. He will probably try to go around it any way he can. Stand close to his head and hold him on a shorter lead and ask him to "come". If he moves only one foot over a log, tire, or onto the bridge, stop, hold him there and give him a reward for his effort.

Then ask for the next foot and if he is willing, let him walk over the obstacle, then reward him again. If he only moves one foot more, reward that and proceed slowly. We don't want him to just run through it. We want him to come when we say "come" and to stop when we say "Whoa". You are beginning to establish a verbal communication with your donkey, so keep it simple and consistent. Do all obstacles the same way.

Donkeys like to step crooked over obstacles. When he has learned to step through, or over an obstacle, but is not going straight, you can step directly in front of him, holding the halter on both sides and ask for straightness as he negotiates the obstacle.

Training for shows

Once he has learned to follow you over and around obstacles, he will be ready to begin the fundamentals of showmanship. Hold your lead in your left hand, keeping your right hand free and straight out in front of you. He should learn to lead with slack in the lead and to follow your shoulder. If he gets too close, you can use your right hand to push him back into position. Once you have begun showmanship training, always lead him this way. Teach him to stand squarely on all fours every time he stops. We are not just teaching him to step up, but to carry his body in a balanced fashion so he will develop good posture and balance.

When you want to teach him to trot on the lead, give the verbal command "trot" and slowly move your own legs into a very slow trot. If he is difficult, do not go to the whip. Try to find something toward which he wants to trot. Above all, don't get discouraged if he won't trot the first few times, just slow back down and do something he already knows, quit that day and try again the next.

Eventually, he will get it. Learn to reward even the slightest movement in the direction of compliance and allow him to progress at his own speed, not yours. Soon he will be wearing his halter and lead, standing tied quietly while you brush him and clean his feet, following you around and over obstacles, loading into a trailer and learning the beginning stages of showmanship. You will have a good, solid foundation on which to begin his formal training.

Chapter 7. The Health Of Your Pet Donkey

It is our experience that donkeys are very stoical by nature. They generally do not show obvious or dramatic signs of illness or lameness until the problem is well advanced. Therefore, familiarity with routine health checks and the behavior of your own donkeys is the key to recognizing problems early.

For both the new and experienced donkey owner, we advise using the following five-point checklist on at least a daily basis:

1. Behavior.
2. Appetite and thirst.
3. Feces and urine.
4. Eyes, nose and resting respiration (breathing).
5. Coat and skin.

Behavior

When monitoring your donkeys' health, observing their behavior is the single most important check. Each donkey will have its own characteristics, e.g. a particular companion, grazing pattern, daily routine and behavior. Sometimes the slightest change indicates a potential problem. Healthy donkeys should be alert and aware, interested in what is going on around them, with their ears pricked. No donkey should spend prolonged periods lying down. Healthy donkeys should be able to get up and down easily and move freely without limping, taking their weight equally on all four legs. Small changes in normal behavior are often the first signs of illness, so get to know your donkeys' behavior as soon as possible.

Appetite and thirst

Donkeys will naturally graze for long periods of time. It is therefore important to control their diet to prevent obesity. Healthy donkeys should be looking to eat throughout the day and have no problem chewing or swallowing. You should, however, be aware that sick donkeys can appear to eat without actually consuming any food. This is known as 'sham eating'. Observe your donkeys carefully to establish whether they are eating normally.

Water

The amount donkeys drink varies according to the air temperature, the moisture content of food, workload, etc. Routinely check your donkeys' water trough for evidence of their normal intake. Sufficient water intake is vital to health and digestion, especially for older, less active donkeys. Therefore, ensuring good water intake is one of the most important elements to keeping your donkey healthy. To ensure good water intake, provide several sources of clean, fresh water at the appropriate height, using, for example, buckets, water troughs or automatic drinkers. In cooler weather, donkeys often reduce their intake of cold water, so offer your donkey warmed water (just with the chill taken off is fine).

If you can't use a warm tap, add some warm water from a kettle to a bucket of water. It may take time for your donkeys to realize warm water is available, so persevere for a week or two and monitor your donkeys' preferences.

Feces and urine

Check for fresh feces, the consistency of which may alter with the diet. There should be a regular output of normal, moist feces formed into balls, which break up easily. Male and female donkeys each adopt a different characteristic stance when urinating. Normal urine is yellow and watery, and may on occasions be cloudy. It should be passed freely, without straining. You should keep a close eye on any donkey that repeatedly attempts to pass urine, or passes urine which is obviously discolored or bloody. Mares in season may be seen to attempt to pass urine more frequently.

Eyes, Nose and Resting Respiration

Eyes should be clean and bright, open and free from discharge. The nostrils should also be clean and discharge-free. At rest, there should be minimal movement of the nostrils as the donkey breathes. In fact, it is often difficult to make out the movements of the chest at rest; the movements of the flanks are often the easiest to observe. A flaring of the nostrils, a marked rise and fall of the ribs and flanks, or any noise associated with a donkey's respiration are causes for further investigation. Exercise, stress, excitement and fever will increase the rate and depth of respiration.

Coat and Skin

A healthy donkey should have a flat, clean coat with no signs of itching, bald areas, sores or abnormal lumps and bumps. It is a good idea to get your donkey used to you routinely running your hands over all areas of the body, legs, head, and sheath or udder area. A donkey's coat can often hide developing problems.

Wounds

If your donkey has a wound, the first step you should take is to prevent further injury. Catch the donkey and calm it. If your donkey is frightened, ensure your own safety when handling it. Always take care when examining wounds, especially those on the limbs.

Seek veterinary advice for any of the following issues:

- Excessive bleeding (hemorrhage). Wounds on the lower legs can bleed profusely. Apply a pressure bandage before calling the vet - for example, bandage firmly with gauze pads to stem the flow of blood.

- Penetration or puncture through the entire skin thickness.

- A wound close to a joint.

- A severe wound.

- Wound contamination such as from dirt or other material.

- Bruises, lumps, swelling and inflammation. In the absence of an obvious wound, these might be the result of an underlying problem. If your donkeys are not up to date with their tetanus vaccinations, they may require a tetanus antitoxin injection and booster vaccination, so you should contact your vet.

You should check each of these five points once a day. If you are concerned that all is not well, there are a number of simple tests and checks that you can do yourself. These will certainly help in giving your vet a full picture of the problem should you feel it necessary to seek further advice.

Additional health checks

- Temperature, pulse, respiration rate (TPR).

- Gut sounds.

- Feed test.

- Condition score and weight.

- Temperature. Adult range normal values: 36.5 to 37.7°C (97.2 to 100°F), average 37.1°C (98.8°F). Young donkey, up to two years old normal values: 36.6 to 38.9°C (97.8 to 102.1°F). Donkeys are individuals and their normal temperature will vary. We recommend taking your donkeys' temperature five or six times over the course of a week at different times of day, and recording the results. This way you will get both yourself and your donkeys used to this procedure, and you'll have a record of your donkeys' normal temperature range, should a problem arise.

Pulse Rate

Normal range: 31 to 53 beats/min. Average: 41 beats/min. With a little practice, anyone can learn to count the pulse in the artery that runs under and across the donkey's lower jaw. Put a hand above the muzzle to keep the donkey's head still. Use the fingertips of your other hand to locate the artery (about 4 mm in diameter). By varying the pressure you will soon be aware of the pulsations corresponding to each heartbeat. Count the number of pulses felt in 15 seconds and multiply by 4 to get your final rate. Getting to know what is normal for your donkey is very important so that you can recognize and compare any changes.

Respiratory Rate

Normal range: 13 to 31 inspiration/min. Average: 20 inspiration/min. It is best to measure the respiratory rate before you take the donkey's temperature or pulse. Stand back to one side and either watch the rise and fall of the flank or, on a cold day, watch the breath coming out of the nostrils. Count the number of breaths in 15 seconds and multiply by 4 (one rise and fall of the flank = one breath). As with the temperature and pulse, it is important that you get to know what is normal for your donkey so that you can recognize and compare any changes.

Gut Sounds

A normal donkey's digestive system is generally a noisy affair, with many squeaks, gurgles and rumbles. These are particularly evident when the grazing is good but are also audible on winter rations (hay and straw). Your vet will use a stethoscope to hear these sounds but you should pick up some of them by placing your own ear against the skin of the flanks (between the last rib and the hind leg). However, take great care because the donkey might kick, particularly if it is in pain. Get used to the normal sounds of a healthy donkey's digestive system as any changes are a good indication of colic (abdominal pain).

Feed Test

A favorite test is the 'ginger biscuit test', although many donkeys will take a biscuit, particularly if they are used to this treatment. A lack of interest is a definite cause for concern.

Weight Loss

Measure your donkeys' weight monthly using either livestock scales or the heart girth measurement, and keep a record. Sudden, unexpected changes in weight can indicate a problem. As a donkey ages, it might naturally lose weight, but this needs to be carefully monitored and feeding and veterinary advice sought before the donkey becomes underweight.

When to call the vet

If you see changes in behavior or suspect that your donkey is unwell, call your vet immediately. Give the vet any information that you have, together with the symptoms the donkey is showing. Monitor the donkey's condition and behavior while you are waiting. It will be really helpful if you can tell the vet if the donkey produces any dung and whether it looks normal. Do not attempt to treat the donkey yourself or give any drugs. Treatment depends on your vet's diagnosis. Your donkeys will also require the following routine treatments to help maintain their health:

- Parasite tests and treatment in accordance with guidelines from the attending vet.

- Hoof trimming every 6–10 weeks as advised by your farrier or vet.

- Vaccinations against flu (annually) and tetanus (every other year).

- Annual dental checks; older donkeys and donkeys with teeth problems may require more regular checks.

Common donkey ailments

1. Colic

Colic is a symptom rather than a disease and is defined as abdominal pain. Donkeys with colic might only become dull and unwilling to eat. Research indicates that a significant percentage of donkeys reported to the veterinary departments as being 'dull' are diagnosed with colic. The stoic nature of donkeys is such that signs of colic are usually less dramatic than those seen in horses, such as rolling, sweating, and pawing the ground. Just because the signs can be less dramatic, it does not mean the donkey is feeling any less pain.

Causes of colic

There are many causes of colic, such as:

- Feed, e.g. sudden changes to diet, poor quality feed, too much grass, feeding cereals.
- Inadequate/dirty water supply.
- Eating non-food items such as plastic bags, rope and bedding.
- Ingestion of poisonous plants.
- Sandy soil.
- Dental disease.

- Worms.
- Stomach ulcers.

Symptoms of Colic

Any of the following signs should cause concern:

- Change in normal behavior.
- Dullness; this is most commonly the first sign.
- Lack of appetite or refusing to eat.
- Unusual, repeated patterns of lying down and getting up.
- Fast breathing, increased heart rate.
- Excessive sweating.
- Changed color of gums or inside the eyelids; a brick red color is a poor sign.
- Lack of or fewer than normal droppings.
- Rolling and pawing at the ground; this is rare in donkeys and should be taken to indicate a very serious problem. It is essential that you are familiar with how your donkeys look when they are in normal health. Observe your donkeys daily, looking for any changes in behavior. Know what normal dung looks like. Be aware of the average number of piles of droppings your donkeys pass each day.

Colic is potentially dangerous because by the time donkeys let you know they have colic, it might be too late to save them.

2. Hyperlipemia

Hyper (too much) lip (id) (fat) aemia (in the blood). All donkey owners should be aware of this condition, as it carries a high risk of death, even when recognized and treated promptly. Donkeys (as well as some native pony breeds) are particularly susceptible to this devastating condition. When donkeys stop eating enough they go into a state of 'negative energy balance', which means that more energy is used up than is taken in.

However, the essential organs still require a food supply, so the body tries to use energy that is stored as fat deposits. The result is that free fatty acids are circulated to the liver to be converted to glucose for use by the body. This system is controlled by complex hormonal events, which should shut down the amount of fat released from fat stores as the liver produces the glucose for the body.

However, donkeys and small ponies are not able to efficiently turn off this fat release, and the blood soon carries excess fat in the circulation. Large amounts of fat cause the liver and kidneys to degenerate and fail, and eventually all the organs in the body fail. The result is irreversible organ damage and death.

Causes of hyperlipemia

Donkeys are more at risk if they:

- Have any underlying disease such as dental problems, colic, a heavy worm burden or choke.
- Are female.
- Are pregnant or lactating mares.
- Have lost significant weight in the preceding weeks.
- Are overweight.
- Are stressed, which causes them to reduce their food intake. Stress can be brought on by pain, loss of a companion,

sudden dietary change, transport, social mixing, bad weather, or sudden weight loss.

Symptoms of hyperlipemia

- Because donkeys are stoic by nature, this illness, like others, might only manifest as a general dullness in the donkey, along with a reduced appetite.

- Subtle changes in behavior are very important early indicators of possible disease. It is important to know how your donkey normally looks and behaves so you can spot any subtle changes.

- Halitosis (bad breath) might be evident.

- There might be reduced production of dung, or production of mucous-covered dung.

Respiratory Diseases

Donkeys are susceptible to the same respiratory diseases as horses. However, as donkeys are very stoic and tend not to be athletic, it is easy to miss the signs and disease might progress significantly before it is noticed.

Causes of respiratory disease

- Infections
- Allergies
- Fibrosis

- Tumors
- Tracheal narrowing/collapse.

Signs of respiratory disease

- Nostrils flaring with each inhalation.

- Excessive abdominal movements.

- An outstretched neck or very noisy respiration.

- Persistent coughing.

- Any nasal discharge, whether thick or thin.

- Abnormal swellings, especially between the bones of the lower jaw and throat area, which could indicate swollen lymph glands as a result of infection.

- Reduced appetite and/or high temperature.

It is essential that you know what is normal for your donkeys. Get used to checking their respiration rate. Donkeys generally breathe in and out between 13 and 31 times per minute (average 20 times per minute).

Reducing the Risk

Ensure your donkeys are vaccinated against equine influenza — this requires an annual booster. Even if your donkeys never leave the paddock, they are still at risk. Other equines might be in the vicinity and could spread infection. You could even bring infection in yourself.

Common Skin Conditions

There are many causes of skin problems in donkeys and it is very important to receive a correct diagnosis from your vet and to follow their recommendations for treatment. Do not be tempted to treat donkeys yourself, as this can delay correct treatment and potentially make the condition worse. Always consult your vet.

1. Problems caused by flies

There are many types of fly including the common housefly, the stable fly, horse flies and the bot fly.

Symptoms

The first signs of irritation by flies include:

- Excessive tail swishing

- Rubbing

- Stamping feet

- Head tossing or shaking

- In some donkeys, fly bites cause raised lumps, and spots of blood might be seen. In the summer, flies can cause great distress and irritation.

Causes

- They can spread infection, especially around the eyes.

- They can lay eggs in wounds.

- Some donkeys suffer large swellings when bitten.

Here are some practical ways to prevent flies from bothering your donkeys:

- Remove manure frequently from grazing paddocks and the stable.
- Keep the stable environment clean; wash and disinfect the stable walls on a weekly basis, remove unwanted feed and clean water troughs.
- Provide a field shelter. This will offer protection whilst the donkeys are in a paddock where they can rest and take refuge from the sun.
- Try to locate shelters in a shady and breezy location.
- Muck heaps should be positioned as far away from stables as possible.
- Use fly strips or traps in the stable and shelter, and remember to hang them well out of reach of the donkeys.
- Summer sheets or fly rugs can help alleviate irritation by preventing flies from landing on the donkeys.

- Use fly fringes or masks that can be worn whilst the donkeys are grazing. The masks are also a useful way to prevent sunburn in pale-skinned donkeys

2. Midges

Culicoides midges cause the condition 'sweet-itch' in hypersensitive (or allergic) donkeys. Midges are very active at dawn and dusk and their bites cause intense irritation to donkeys, leading to excess rubbing, especially on the mane and tail areas. The sore areas often bleed, attracting more insects. Symptoms are similar to those stated above.

In addition, it is important to:

- Stable donkeys at dawn and dusk.
- Use fly repellents several times a day.
- Keep donkeys away from water courses and wet areas where midges congregate.
- If your donkey is affected by sweet-itch, seek the advice of your vet.

3. Mites

There are a number of mites that cause intense irritation. Some types live on donkeys, while others live in hay and straw. They cause irritation by biting, usually on the lower legs or around the head and neck. Your vet might be able to find these on skin samples. Various insecticide preparations are available.

4. Lice

Lice are parasites that live and lay eggs on their equine host. There are two types of lice found commonly in donkeys: chewing lice which eat scurf and dead skin in the coat, and sucking lice that feed on the blood of their host.

Symptoms

Both types of lice can cause:
- Itching
- Rubbing
- Hair loss
- Depression
- In the case of sucking lice, anemia.

Causes

Lice are more common in the winter months and tend to prefer animals with long coats and those with lowered immunity (eg the very young or old, or donkeys who are sick). Lice live within the donkey coat and are commonly seen in the armpits and above the eye socket.

Eggs, immature 'nymphs' and adults might all be seen and should be included in the treatment program. Thankfully, lice are host-specific, so lice on your donkeys cannot pass to humans or non-equine animals.

Treatment of lice can be difficult and might require more than one application. We recommend that you seek advice from a vet as many of the traditional 'anti-lice' preparations have disappointing success rates in the thick donkey coat.

5. Ticks

Ticks are parasites that bite and feed on the blood of a mammalian host before falling off to complete their lifecycle. Ticks tend to be common in areas with long grass and bracken, such as the New Forest, and moorland. Although the tick bite itself rarely causes more than local irritation, ticks are a problem due to their ability to pass on infectious disease to equines and other mammals.

The most well known of these is Lymes Disease which can cause severe illness in mammals including donkeys, horses and humans. It is important to be vigilant and check your donkeys over for ticks in spring, summer and autumn, particularly when they are grazing in high-risk areas with long grass. Common areas for attachment are in between the back legs, under the tail and in the ears. If ticks are found, they must be carefully removed so that the mouth part is not left in the animal.

Special 'tick removers' are perfect for the job and available from any veterinary practice. Avoid traditional methods of tick removal, including burning, squeezing or smothering in Vaseline, as they increase the risk of the tick regurgitating its stomach contents into the animal, thus increasing the risk of infection.

Parasites

Intestinal parasites affecting donkeys are similar to those that affect horses. These include nematodes (large and small strongyles, ascarids, pinworms), bots, and Cestodes (tapeworms). Basic principles of parasite control are the same as for larger equines. Medications used with success in donkeys include fenbendazole, ivermectin, albendazole, and pyrantel pamoate.

Lungworms

Animals in certain areas of the country are also affected by lungworms. These areas are not well defined. Donkeys are the natural hosts for lungworms and as such do not show obvious signs of disease when infected. In fact, the incidence of donkey infestation is not known. Mules are reported to be relatively unaffected by lungworm infestation, much like donkeys. Horses, however, may be severely affected, exhibiting coughing and wheezing. Lungworms should be suspected if an affected horse is pastured with donkeys or mules.

Definitive diagnosis is made by demonstrating the presence of Dictyocaulis arnfeldi larvae in fresh feces. Treatment is achieved by oral dosing with ivermectin, followed by a repeat treatment in three weeks. Other strategies of parasite control include pasture rotation, removal of manure, and deworming of new herd additions. Successful use or need for deworming medications should be measured by periodic fecal examinations. I recommend the sugar centrifugation technique of fecal analysis.

Worming

Donkeys should be wormed every two to three months with an equine paste wormer. Until recently, rotational worming with an ivermectin product then a fenbendazole or other category of wormers was the preferred worming technique. This is thought to prevent the donkey from developing immunity to wormers. It is still used quite often. Many vets now advise staying with an ivermectin product throughout the year but using a fenbendazole or other non-ivermectin product for one or two applications before you resume treatment with the ivermectin.

Whatever your worming schedule, you must use an ivermectin product after the first and last frost to prevent bots. Bot eggs can survive in the cold. Consult your vet and follow his or her recommendations on worming. We practice rotational worming with an ivermectin (trade names Zimecterin, Equimectrin or Equalan) and a fenbendazole (trade names SafeGuard or Panacur). These can be found at feed stores, co-ops, veterinary offices, vet supply retailers, or mail order catalogs such as Jeffers and Horse.com.

Foals are wormed at two months with a product that protects against roundworms, which are more common in foals and young animals. You will notice that your young foal will eat mom's poop off the ground. Don't panic. Although it can lead to worms, it's primarily nature's way of immunizing him. Both people and donkeys need some exposure to bacteria to stimulate the immune system to perform. Wormers are safe and effective as long as you follow the instructions on the box and use the correct dosage. Underdosing is as good as not worming at all and will result in poor parasite control.

Overdosing could also be problematic. After placing the wormer in the back of your donkey's mouth, give them a bite or two of feed, grain, or cookie to make them swallow the paste and not spit it out, which some will do. I hold their heads until I know they've swallowed it. Don't give too much or they may choke. You may also try spreading the wormer on a slice of bread and giving them a "medicine sandwich". Some of ours have gotten wise to that trick though!

Carrots and garlic are natural wormers and should be included in the diet.

Vaccinations

We vaccinate all donkeys once a year (preferably March or April) at the beginning of the fly season. We vaccinate for Eastern and Western encephalomyelitis, tetanus, and influenza. This shot is sometimes called a 5-way. We also give a rabies shot once a year. Pregnant jennies receive a rhinopneumonitis injection (commonly Rhino-Pneumabort K) in the 5th, 7th, and 9th months of pregnancy to prevent abortion. Our show donkeys are given a Rhino-flu booster 3 weeks prior to attending a show and are isolated from the rest of the herd for at least 2 weeks following a show.

This is done to prevent them from becoming a carrier and spreading any virus they may have picked up from the show to the herd. We also vaccinate our jennets 30 days before foaling in order for her to be at peak immunity and to trigger the immune system of the foal. Consult your veterinarian as to their thoughts regarding what vaccinations are appropriate for your area and your breeding program. Foals should receive a tetanus antitoxin injection at birth. Foals are given their first vaccination at four months, a booster 30 days later, and then a booster annually.

There is much discussion about the West Nile Virus and whether or not to give that vaccination to donkeys. From many discussions with several veterinarians in private practice and at Texas A&M

University, I've discovered that the veterinary community endorses giving the West Nile vaccine as opposed to not giving it.

The mortality rate for those animals that become infected is 30%, which is high. It is suggested that you give this vaccination to jennets that are not pregnant. If you must give it to a pregnant jennet, do not give it in the 1st or last trimester of her pregnancy in order to prevent misscarriage or other complications. Consult your veterinarian to see if the West Nile vaccine is something he or she suggests for you.

It is not difficult to learn how to give your own injections. Have your vet instruct you, but be sure you know where and how to give the injection before attempting to administer your own shots. We use a 20 gauge, " needle for adults and a 20 gauge, 1/2" needle for foals. Be very careful giving shots to foals, especially in the neck. The area to receive the injection is very small and located close to the spinal cord on top and the jugular vein on bottom. It's better to give a foal an injection in the muscle in their rear. Seek instructions from your vet before giving your own shots. Always let the vet administer an injection in the vein; never try that yourself.

Always keep an un-expired syringe of Epinephrine handy if you give your own injections. Although extremely rare, anaphylactic shock can occur after any type of injection is administered. Anaphylactic shock is a severe allergic reaction to some antigen introduced to the body in an injection or bite. This is very dangerous and will constrict the airway and cause death quite quickly.

If the donkey is going to go into anaphylactic shock, it will occur within minutes of giving the animal an injection, but can be reversed immediately with Epinephrine. I never give an injection then leave the animal. I stay with them for at least 10 minutes then I check them again within the first hour of giving any injection. Donkeys can have reactions to injections up to an hour after administering the injection. The good news is that although frightening to the owner, reactions are not common.

Donkeys are vaccinated with the same products as full-size equines and at the same frequencies. However, there have been no conclusive studies regarding the effectiveness or safety of equine products in donkeys. I was involved in a limited vaccination trial (unpublished study) with a small number of miniature donkeys. Titers were evaluated after vaccination with commercially available equine products against Eastern and Western encephalitis, equine herpes virus1 and 4, equine influenza virus type A1 and A2, and Potomac horse fever (PHF).

Results were inconclusive yet donkeys responded to these vaccines in the majority of instances as demonstrated by increasing titers, except for the PHF vaccine. (While only one brand of PHF vaccine was used, I still recommend vaccination against PHF in at-risk geographical locations.)

Some owners and veterinarians have suggested that miniature equines should be vaccinated with reduced doses of the standard equine vaccines. I do not recommend this practice, as there is no scientific evidence for it and, in fact, the lower dose may not stimulate the immune system sufficiently to provide a protective response. No vaccine challenge studies have been or are likely to be performed in donkeys.

Since 150-pound equine foals and 2000-pound draft horses are given the same dose of vaccine, I recommend full-size, standard equine vaccine doses for donkeys of all sizes. The specific vaccines used should be selected based on the disease risks in a particular location and the risk of infection from new arrivals and/or exposure at shows and events. This is particularly true for equine respiratory diseases.

No data is available regarding the incidence of equine herpes virus abortion in donkeys, therefore, the practice of vaccinating donkeys at 5, 7, and 9 months of pregnancy has been questioned. Some owners have reported a high incidence of side effects with these vaccines and even blamed abortions on their use, but to my knowledge, there is no concrete evidence to support this. I have limited experience with the use of vaccines protective against West Nile virus and no experience with those for Venezuelan equine encephalitis or equine protozoal myelitis (EPM). To date, there have been no reported adverse effects from use of WNV vaccine in donkeys, although it is unlikely that any manufacturer will test vaccine effectiveness specifically in donkeys.

The EPM vaccine is no longer available, and unless a donkey resides along the Mexican border, there may not be a reason for administering the Venezuelan equine encephalitis vaccine.

Chapter 8. Miniature Donkey Reproduction

Breeding and raising miniature donkeys is lots of fun and is much less stressful than dealing with horses. They are considered of breeding age at three to four years old and can foal into their twenties. There is usually very little, if any, veterinary involvement in breeding donkeys. Because of their size, most breeders don't routinely do pre or post foaling exams or ultrasound exams.

Breeding fees are typically in the $300/£231-$500/£385 range with top animals commanding up to $1000/£770. These fees usually include "mare care" so typically this is the only cost to breed. Those of you who have broodmares know that the breeding fee is often only the beginning of the story. Not with donkeys.

Miniature donkeys conceive and foal easily and are generally comfortable with sharing a newborn foal with their owner; the foals are often friendly at birth or shortly thereafter. I am a tad biased but I think there are few things cuter than a baby donkey. They weigh about twenty pounds, range in size from 18" to 24" at birth, and will climb right up in your lap if let them. The decision to breed comes with a responsibility.

There is a difference between a wonderful pet and an animal worthy of adding to the miniature donkey gene pool. A conscientious breeder breeds the best jennet he/she can afford to a high quality jack, even if the intention is to produce "only a pet". Today's breeding animals provide the gene pool of the future. Donkeys live a long time and who can say what decisions will be made down the line and breeding "only pets" is not good for the future of miniature donkeys. If you are new to genetic principals and husbandry it would be helpful to you to find a knowledgeable, responsible breeder to ask questions. Most breeders are happy to assist.

Reproductive physiology and behavior – The Estrus Cycle

The estrus cycle length in donkeys is 21-28 days, with the jennet sexually receptive for 5-10 days of this period. The ovulatory follicle size is similar to that in full-sized equines and follicles bigger than 25-30 mm in diameter should be considered potentially ovulatory. One miniature jennet I examined ovulated a 42 mm diameter follicle. The cervical appearance changes with the stage of the estrus cycle, relaxing during estrus, which is accompanied by an increase in vaginal mucous secretions. Jennets may cycle throughout the winter.

Reproductive behavior

A jennet often shows her first heat at 8-12 months of age. Female receptivity is evidenced by the jennet backing up to the jack and making jawing motions with the mouth. Jennets in estrus will kick a jack in the chest (and face if the jack is not careful) for several minutes when receptive. This behavior is required for the jack to achieve a full erection. Receptive jennets also squat, wink the vulva, and urinate in the presence of the jack. A receptive jennet may also raise her tail when approached by a jack. Jennets mount each other on occasion, with the estrus jennet on the bottom.

Some jennets do not show receptivity when there is no jack present, when nursing a foal, or when another female interferes with the advances of the jack. A jack pursues a jennet in estrus, sometimes very aggressively, and especially when first introduced. He may bite the neck, back, and hind legs and even draw blood. As a consequence, some jacks have to wear a breeding muzzle to avoid injury to the jennet. Jacks usually calm down after a short time (15-30 minutes) and then the muzzle may be removed. It is easy to teach most jacks to mount without biting the jennet by using a chain lead shank over the nose. Vigorous jerking motions on the chain along with verbal commands usually result in a quick learning process for the jack. Donkeys are intelligent animals and respond well to consistent, firm training methods.

A jennet may back up to the jack after ovulation, but he may not mount again if he has recently bred the jennet by natural cover or through the collection for artificial insemination. Normally, jacks mount jennets a few times before fully erect, and some jacks are slow to achieve an erection (10-15 minutes). There is no correlation between time to achieve full erection or degree of aggressive breeding behavior and fertility. The jack responds to a jennet's jawing behavior with vocalization. Some jacks are timid and will not breed when new people are present. It is common for multiple mounts to be required, along with some periods of inactivity at a short distance from the jennet, before the jack achieves a full erection and completes the breeding.

Field breeding

Jack owners most commonly use field breeding by turning one jack out with as many as 10 jennets. The jack selects the most receptive jennet to breed by checking the herd's manure for pheromones that may be involved in estrus detection. Receptive jennets may also approach a breeding pair to attract the jack.

Hand breeding

Controlled, hand or "appointment" breeding allows for the recording of exact breeding dates. The breeding cycle may be coordinated with serial transrectal ultrasound examinations of the ovaries to determine the time of ovulation and the best time to breed. Jacks may be overly aggressive or timid when first training them to mount in controlled situations; however, they are fast learners. Estrus synchronization protocols useful in horses seem to be effective in the donkey. If hand breeding is used it is suggested that the jennet be bred on the second day of estrus and then at 48-hour intervals until the end of the heat.

Artificial Insemination

Artificial insemination (AI) is possible on the farm or with transported fresh, cooled semen. Jacks are easy to train for collection, although this technique is not currently used on a widespread basis. Donkey semen is very concentrated and in general has good fertility. It can be handled similar to that of the stallion, and skim milk extenders seem to be useful to keep sperm alive during transport in artificial insemination programs. French workers have published freezing protocols for donkey semen.

Summary

The reproductive anatomy of the male donkey is similar to that of the standard horse. The same applies for the female, including the size of the reproductive tract. Female donkeys have a 21-28 day estrus cycle with obvious behavioral signs of receptivity when a jack is present. Lactation may stop a donkey from cycling while other females (related or not) may interfere with displays of sexual receptivity and breeding. Pasture and hand breeding are both used in donkeys. Artificial insemination can be performed successfully in donkeys although not widely accepted by owners at this time.

Transrectal and transabdominal ultrasound are safe and effective methods for reproductive.

Before you allow a jennet to conceive on our farm, we consider many things for the welfare of the jennet and the little foal. Conscientious breeders should always have the jennet and foal's future and welfare in mind before breeding. The state of the economy should be considered. Here is the process you should adopt over time:

- Identify positive traits by observing the jennets conformation and personality.

- Evaluate and research the jennet's and jack's pedigrees to select the positive traits from each and avoid possible inbreeding.

- Select the sire that will best improve upon the jennet's traits. Choose a jack to enhance and complement the selected jennet's qualities.

- Breed no jennet under 29", avoiding trends relating only to small size and complications or death during delivery. (The National Miniature Donkey Association Breed Standard states "under 30 inches").

- Breed for conformation, avoiding trends/fads relating to color. Color is the icing on the cake but should not be the sole and primary breeding objective. If you are looking at breeding from a marketing approach, remember the market is fickle. If you breed for all blacks and the market supports traditional grays, sales may decline leaving your foals unplaced.

- Observe the jennet's health and breed only healthy animals. The health of the foal directly correlates to the mother's health at the time of conception and throughout the one-year pregnancy.

- Breed only after the age of three. Many jennets may not be good mothers if bred too young and may abort near term. They are "teenagers" until three years of age.

- Breed only if there is a likely placement for the foal. Consider the economy. Breeding fewer is always better than more. Keeping the supply down consistently places animals in good homes and keeps the market demand up. Too many breeders breeding too many donkeys can cause a statewide marketing problem. While this may create opportunities for the buyer, some animals may be left without placement. Sale prices will decrease when the supply is above demand.

- Sell only if there is placement in a good home with another donkey. Consider a two for one price. Some breeders will give a second donkey to a customer who can afford only one to ensure a pair of donkeys in a good, caring home.

- Geld jack foals, unless they are of superior quality and selected to be a herd sire. Make the decision by six months; the appropriate gelding age.

- Take a critical look at your jennet, or have an equine vet do so, to determine her conformation faults. Better yet, have her inspected at four years old or over to know whether she is of sufficient quality to enter the stud book. If she does not pass with 65% or higher, it is probably not wise to breed from her.

- If she is an older jennet, age ten or over, with no known previous breeding history, discuss with your vet the merits and problems likely to arise from breeding such an older animal. Foal rejection is one problem that can often occur in older mares or jennets that have never previously produced a live foal.

- Have a vet examine the jennet's reproductive tract to see if it is normal and healthy. There are recorded cases of jennets that look perfectly normal on the exterior and even cycled normally but never conceived a foal. Internal examinations proved that there was no connection between the vagina and the uterus. The abnormality left the vagina as a blind pouch and semen could never ever reach its destination.

- For the sake and sanity of both jack and jennet owner, consider the jennet's education. Is she halter trained and easy to catch? Does she stand willingly to have her hooves trimmed? Does she load and travel in a trailer with no problems? While this type of basic education may seem irrelevant to the breeding process, it is vital should the jennet need to be removed from the pasture in case of an accident, at the time of farrier work, or if the jack owner uses in-hand breeding methods or equine artificial insemination.

- Should the jack owner utilize the ultrasound technology of the local vet to verify pregnancy, the jennet may need to be taken to the vet clinic. If the jack owner is expected to give the jennet the basic education she should have received at home, don't be surprised if a training fee is added to the bill. Basic training should already have been completed at home before sending the jennet away for breeding.

- Visit the owner of the jack to whom you plan to send your jennet. Talk extensively with the owner about methods of breeding (in-hand, pasture or artificial insemination), take a tour of the facilities, and discuss feeding and management of the donkeys there and any special needs your jennet may have.

- Jennets are also requested to be dewormed, have hooves trimmed, and 4-way shots prior to coming to the farm for breeding. If you are comfortable with the facilities and management, then meet the jack. Is he registered and inspected?

- What was his grade at inspection? Does he have a show record at halter or performance? If he is a large standard or mammoth, ask if he is a jennet jack or a mule jack.

- Does it matter if the jack is a jennet jack or a mule jack? Not really, at least not on the exterior, but behaviorally speaking there can be a huge difference! A jennet has been raised to breed jennets and will readily accept them. Even so, if pasture breeding is used there can be the considerable hassle of the jennet and chasing around. A few jacks will breed both horse mares and jennets, but most develop a strong preference depending on how they were raised. A mule jack, however, has been raised with horses with the goal in mind that he breeds horse mares for mule production. He looks like a donkey on the outside but he thinks like a horse on the inside. Because he doesn't think he is a donkey, he will behave more like a horse stallion and he may attack and savage any jennet presented to him for breeding.

- If a jennet is turned loose with such a jack she can be badly bitten and beaten, and it may take four or five grown men to drive him off and rescue her. The consequence of such traumatization can be that the jennet is terrified of being approached, never mind breed by any jack in the future.

- Seriously question any thought of breeding a donkey in the fall or winter months unless a heated barn is available for cold weather foaling. Donkeys can foal after gestation periods of 11-14 months so it is easy for all but the most vigilant owner to miss the right time. Winter foaling in a snow bank can be fatal, or at the very least result in frozen ears, tails, or limbs. Generally, foals produced in April - August, depending on the provincial location, do best because they have the advantage of the sunshine and fresh grass.

- Jennets may cycle erratically throughout a sunny winter, but may not ovulate because like all equines this time of year is a period of anestrous which gives them a reproductive rest. With careful selection of both parents and time of year for breeding, the resulting offspring should surpass both parents inequality and arrive at the best time of year for optimum growth and development.

- Breeding donkeys may seem as simple as the equation of one jennet plus one jack will produce a fuzzy, long eared foal next year. However, donkeys are part of the equine family and as such, the breeder has a choice of three basic breeding methods:

Foaling out the jennet

Spring is almost here and with the change of seasons comes foaling time for equine breeders. During the last quarter of pregnancy, we all play the waiting game.

Throughout pregnancy, the jennets have maintained a quiet lifestyle with regular exercise, but no hard or fast work, up until the last quarter of pregnancy (3 months). The last quarter should involve some exercise at liberty, but no riding or driving. A program of regular hoof care (every 6-8 weeks) and deworming have prepared the jennet to be in good condition for foaling.

However, it is wise to check with the vet before any deworming medication is given during the last quarter of gestation. Changes in the feed are usually not required until the last quarter of gestation when the fetus makes the greatest growth.

Excessive feed early in pregnancy can create obesity and potential foaling problems. Increased feed for the jennet should be maintained from the final quarter of pregnancy throughout the first three months of foaling. The latter is the period of maximum milk production.

This is the time when protein, vitamin and mineral levels such as calcium and phosphorus need to be increased to accommodate the great physical drain on the jennet during this six months of hard work. It is wise to seek an advice from an equine nutritionist or veterinarian regards the important dietary changes during this period.

Having the previous year's breeding date on the jennet greatly assists in establishing a foaling date for this year. Therefore, it is crucial to know every jennet in the herd well and keep good records for the signs shown with each foaling.

We have found that the average donkey gestation period lasts twelve months plus or minus one week. Then there are those jennets that choose to foal anywhere from 11 months to 14 months - all within the normal range of gestation for donkeys. The same jennet is rarely consistent in the length of gestation time from one pregnancy to the next.

Jennets are also rarely consistent in showing the same signs of impending birth from one pregnancy to the next.

However, generally a jennet will show some or all of the following signs:

- Gradual enlargement of the udder from about 30 days prior to birth. As the birth date approaches the udder becomes enlarged and remains enlarged.

- Enlargement of the teats to the very trip occurs several days prior to birth.

- A waxy secretion that forms a cap over the end of each teat may form up to 48 hours prior to birth. Some jennets actually drip milk in the last 24-48 hours. Under no circumstances milk the jennet at this stage.

- Softening of the pelvic ligaments creates a groove along either side of the spinal column in the loin area towards the tail head. This sign may go unnoticed in a maiden jennet or one with a thick winter coat.

- The vulva becomes very soft and loose during the last week or two and gradually elongates as birth approaches. Birth is usually in a matter of hours when the lips of the vulva are swollen out.

- The jennet may show an unfriendly attitude towards other animals and prefer to stand by herself. This attitude is usually prevalent during the last two weeks prior to foaling.

- The jennet will show restlessness as the foal turns and prepares to move into the birth passage. At this stage, she may look thinner, walk around the stall and get up and down a number of times. Sometimes birth occurs immediately after the foal has turned, or sometimes the jennet will wait for another day or so.

- Just prior to birth, the jennet's tail will be carried out away from the body, lifted and usually kinked to one side. She may frequently pass small amounts of soft manure, or urinate.

- Jennets not only show various combinations of signs prior to foaling but unlike horse mares, they can and do foal at any time of the day or night, so close observation is important. In general, we have found that if the jennet shows no signs of foaling by midnight, then she will often wait until the four to six am time frame. Yet she may also choose to foal at noon, supper time or while you are doing morning chores! A clean, safely fenced corral or special large clean box stall is ideal for foaling. Foaling out where barbed wire fences surround the pasture, near streams or sloughs or among the rest of the herd can invite disaster.

Chapter 9. Final Thoughts

Are you considering miniature donkeys? Or have you just purchased your first pair? There are a number of things you need to know to be sure you and your new equine will get off to a good start. The first thing you will need is adequate housing and a place for them to be turned out for exercise. The housing should provide protection from rain, snow or sun and be free of drafts. Heat is not necessary, but a tight building is important, especially for those who live in cold climates. A small barn or outbuilding will do nicely depending on the part of the country you live in. In cold climates, you might want something more substantial. The flooring should be appropriate to drain or absorb urine and be easy to clean or "muck out". Stall mats or bedding (straw or sawdust) work well although straw is a better choice for the foaling stall.

The donkeys will need access to fresh, clean water year round (an automatic waterer or a tank heater in cold climates is a real time saver). You will also need a hayrack, mineral and plain salt blocks and a feed tub. Check the stall and paddock area carefully to make sure there are no sharp edges or places an animal can get caught or injured. Ideally, you should have a stall or barn with access to a paddock or pasture which will allow your donkeys to come and go if the weather turns bad and you are not available. This is the best situation for the donkeys and the least labor intensive for you.

If you have purchased your donkeys from an experienced, reputable breeder no doubt they have given you information to get you started. You have probably gathered that a donkey, as a herd animal, needs a companion and the best companion is another donkey. Even if you purchased your miniature donkey as a companion to a horse, what happens when the horse goes off to be ridden? Usually, the horse doesn't want to leave his donkey friends and the donkey is very unhappy to have his companion go without him, so a pair of donkeys makes good sense. A single miniature donkey will be lonely without a companion, often braying and pacing when alone.

Sheep and/or goats are not appropriate companions for a single donkey, since one-on-one donkey/small livestock play could turn rough. The equation may change if you have two miniature donkeys coexisting with smaller livestock. Gradual introductions will let everyone get to know one another and ease transition times.

You will also need to properly introduce dogs as well as other family pets when you bring your new donkeys home. Donkeys tend to have a natural suspicion of dogs (as predators), but with time will get to know family members. Be sure your dogs are not chasing after the donkeys.

Beware of foals for sale that are too young for weaning, as this can affect how well adjusted they will be as adults. The little ones need to stay with their moms for approximately five to six months, but no younger than four months. You might want to ask the person you're buying from if they would keep the foal and jennet together, if the foal is too young, for a little longer. Even though you are eager to get your new pet home, it is in the donkey's best interest and yours. Young foals will learn many valuable lessons by remaining with adult donkeys until weaning.

Every intact miniature donkey jack that isn't being used for breeding should be gelded. Your family will be happier with him as a wonderful, loving pet and his life will be much less complicated without having to deal with hormones. Many ungelded jacks face an uncertain future of being passed from home to home or ending up in an auction due to their instinctive, unbridled passions at times.

You should also make yourself aware of all the potential illnesses that can affect donkeys so that you can make your donkey safe and well by spotting the signs early.

Thank you for buying this book. We hope it will help you on your journey with your new beloved miniature dokey!

Copyright and Trademarks: This publication is Copyrighted 2017 by Zoodoo Publishing. All products, publications, software and services mentioned and recommended in this publication are protected by trademarks. In such instance, all trademarks & copyright belong to the respective owners. All rights reserved. No part of this book may be reproduced or transferred in any form or by any means, graphic, electronic, or mechanical, including photocopying, recording, taping, or by any information storage retrieval system, without the written permission of the authors. Pictures used in this book are either royalty free pictures bought from stock-photo websites or have the source mentioned underneath the picture.

Disclaimer and Legal Notice: This product is not legal or medical advice and should not be interpreted in that manner. You need to do your own due-diligence to determine if the content of this product is right for you. The author and the affiliates of this product are not liable for any damages or losses associated with the content in this product. While every attempt has been made to verify the information shared in this publication, neither the author nor the affiliates assume any responsibility for errors, omissions or contrary interpretation of the subject matter herein. Any perceived slights to any specific person(s) or organization(s) are purely unintentional. We have no control over the nature, content and availability of the web sites listed in this book. The inclusion of any web site links does not necessarily imply a recommendation or endorse the views expressed within them. Zoodoo Publishing takes no responsibility for, and will not be liable for, the websites being temporarily unavailable or being removed from the Internet. The accuracy and completeness of information provided herein and opinions stated herein are not guaranteed or warranted to produce any particular results, and the advice and strategies, contained herein may not be suitable for every individual. The author shall not be liable for any loss incurred as a consequence of the use and application, directly or indirectly, of any information presented in this work. This publication is designed to provide information in regards to the subject matter covered. The information included in this book has been compiled to give an overview of the subjects and detail some of the symptoms, treatments etc. that are available to people with this condition. It is not intended to give medical advice. For a firm diagnosis of your condition, and for a treatment plan suitable for you, you should consult your doctor or consultant. The writer of this book and the publisher are not responsible for any damages or negative consequences following any of the treatments or methods highlighted in this book. Website links are for informational purposes and should not be seen as a personal endorsement; the same applies to the products detailed in this book. The reader should also be aware that although the web links included were correct at the time of writing, they may become out of date in the future.

Printed in Great Britain
by Amazon